Deep Neuro-Fuzzy Systems with Python

With Case Studies and Applications from the Industry

Himanshu Singh
Yunis Ahmad Lone

Apress®

Deep Neuro-Fuzzy Systems with Python

Himanshu Singh
Allahabad, Uttar Pradesh, India

Yunis Ahmad Lone
Hyderabad, Andhra Pradesh, India

ISBN-13 (pbk): 978-1-4842-5360-1
https://doi.org/10.1007/978-1-4842-5361-8

ISBN-13 (electronic): 978-1-4842-5361-8

Managing Director, Apress Media LLC: Welmoed Spahr
Acquisitions Editor: Celestin Suresh John
Development Editor: James Markham
Coordinating Editor: Aditee Mirashi

Cover designed by eStudioCalamar

Cover image designed by Freepik (www.freepik.com)

Distributed to the book trade worldwide by Springer Science+Business Media New York, 233 Spring Street, 6th Floor, New York, NY 10013. Phone 1-800-SPRINGER, fax (201) 348-4505, e-mail orders-ny@springer-sbm.com, or visit www.springeronline.com. Apress Media, LLC is a California LLC and the sole member (owner) is Springer Science + Business Media Finance Inc (SSBM Finance Inc). SSBM Finance Inc is a **Delaware** corporation.

For information on translations, please e-mail rights@apress.com, or visit http://www.apress.com/rights-permissions.

Apress titles may be purchased in bulk for academic, corporate, or promotional use. eBook versions and licenses are also available for most titles. For more information, reference our Print and eBook Bulk Sales web page at http://www.apress.com/bulk-sales.

Any source code or other supplementary material referenced by the author in this book is available to readers on GitHub via the book's product page, located at www.apress.com/978-1-4842-5360-1. For more detailed information, please visit http://www.apress.com/source-code.

Printed on acid-free paper

Table of Contents

TABLE OF CONTENTS

About the Authors

Himanshu Singh is currently an artificial intelligence consultant for ADP Inc. He has six years of experience in the industry, mainly in computer vision and natural language processing. Himanshu has authored three books in the Machine Learning domain. He received his MBA from Narsee Monjee Institute of Management Studies and received his postgraduate diploma in applied statistics.

Yunis Ahmad Lone has more than 22 years of experience in the IT industry, with around 10 years of it in Machine Learning. Currently, Yunis is a PhD researcher at Trinity College, Dublin, Ireland. Yunis completed his bachelor's and master's, both from BITS Pilani. He has held various leadership positions at multi-national corporations, including Tata Consultancy Services, Deloitte, and Fidelity Investments.

About the Technical Reviewer

Mridul Saran is a data scientist with a strong familiarity in various deep neural network architectures, data regularization techniques, and optimization strategies.

He has significant industrial experience in handling data science projects and is currently leading a team that is building a Machine Learning and natural language processing-based business intelligence platform at an IT company based in India.

Starting with raw data exploration and then deriving the descriptive, predictive, and prescriptive stories out of it, Mridul thoroughly enjoys his journey with data. He has spent a good amount of time researching and publishing information about neural networks and looks forward to a world where machines can dream.

Acknowledgments

First of all, I would like to thank my co-author, Mr. Yunis. He is the reason I got the chance to work on the Neuro Fuzzy Inference. Under his leadership, I finished a working prototype for a client using ANFIS. That gave me the boost to initiate this book and let readers know about this field. I would also like to thank Mr. Sadhan Reddy, who helped me with the technical aspects of this book. I would like to thank Shivani, Praveen, and Rajeev (my students), who helped fill in many gaps in this book.

I would like to thank Aditee, the coordinating editor at Apress, who kept on following up with me and guided me with queries. Without her, I would have always fallen behind schedule. I would also like to thank Mr. Celestin John, for providing me with the opportunity to write a book on this topic.

Lastly, I would like to thank my wife, Shikha. Without her, I would have never had the motivation and boost to keep writing this book.

Introduction

This is a textbook for students and professionals who want to know about Fuzzy Networks and their applications in Python. We have tried to explain the topics with examples that readers can understand easily and that make the concepts relevant to real-life scenarios. The initial part of the book talks about Fuzzy Networks, logic, and inference systems. The second half mainly talks about the amalgamation of Deep Learning with Fuzzy Logic. It explores the architectures that are currently used in the industry.

We have tried to keep the level of mathematics as simple as possible, so that the concepts can be understood readily. Readers from mathematical backgrounds and those having prior knowledge of Machine Learning will find it easier to understand, but the book is structured in such a way that even readers without this prior knowledge will not find it overly tough.

We start this book by introducing Fuzzy Sets in Chapter 1. Chapter 2 introduces the concepts of Fuzzy Rules and reasoning and explains membership functions. In Chapter 3, we discuss Fuzzy Inference Systems, which are mainly used to make Fuzzy Control Systems.

In Chapters 4 and 5, we discuss the concepts of Machine Learning and neural networks, which will help you understand the further concepts of Fuzzy Networks. We cover optimization and parameter tuning as well. In Chapter 6, we start discussing Fuzzy Neural Networks and their different architectures and finally, in Chapter 7, we discuss some of the advanced concepts related to Deep Fuzzy Networks.

Overall, this book is written with the intention to make the concept of Fuzzy Networks simple to the readers and they should not only understand the mathematics behind it, but also they should be able to understand the practical implementation in Python.

CHAPTER 1

Introduction to Fuzzy Set Theory

This chapter sets the foundation for the rest of the book. You will be introduced to soft computing and Fuzzy Systems. You will learn about the Classical and Fuzzy Sets and the differences between them. You will then look at the properties of different sets, and you'll learn how different operations can be performed on them. This chapter also includes a basic introduction to membership functions, which are then explained in detail in the next chapter. Wherever required, Python code is provided for execution purposes.

Soft Computing and Fuzzy Systems

When you have crisply defined data that is precise and easy to understand, applying hard computing to it is perfect. Hard computing is based on binary logic, classical sets, crisp (precise) systems and software, basic numerical analysis, etc. But when you try to apply this same approach to real-world problems that include imprecise data—maybe the dataset is partially true, it has a lot of approximations, and so on—hard computing fails. The best way to tackle this situation is to use the soft computing approach.

A very basic example is 2+2. In this scenario, you can use hard computing to arrive at 4. But when you change the equation to 2+x, where

© Himanshu Singh, Yunis Ahmad Lone 2020
H. Singh and Y. A. Lone, *Deep Neuro-Fuzzy Systems with Python*,
https://doi.org/10.1007/978-1-4842-5361-8_1

x ranges from 0 to 5, soft computing always gives better results. Before you move on to understanding exactly what soft computing is, study the flowchart in Figure 1-1. It depicts the difference between hard and soft computing when it comes to problem solving.

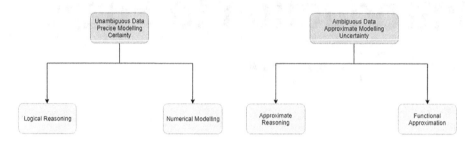

Figure 1-1. *Hard computing versus soft computing*

Soft computing tries to imitate the human mind in order to make decisions. These models have cognitive abilities, which include:

- Ability to think

- Ability to reason

- Ability to organize

- Ability to memorize

- Ability to recognize

- Ability to process

When your data is *imprecise* (it has partial truths and is full of approximations), soft computing is the best approach. The following are features of soft computing-based problem-solving approaches:

- Biologically inspired

- Fault tolerant

- Full of optimizations

- Helps make wiser and more intelligent machines

- Helps in achieving robustness, tractability, and lower costs

- Heavy computation

- Goal driven

Table 1-1 lists the basic constituents of the soft computing approach.

Table 1-1. *Basic Constituents of Soft Computing*

Constituent	Benefits
Neural Networks	To learn and adapt based on uncertainty in data
Fuzzy Set Theory	Knowledge representation
Genetic Algorithms	For efficient searching
Traditional AI	Using mathematical approaches

Now that you have read about the basics of soft computing, turn your attention to understanding Fuzzy Systems. Fuzzy Systems are one of the core parts of soft computing, so you need to understand them. Fuzzy Systems, along with soft computing, make a very strong foundation for an inference system, also called an *Adaptive Neuro-Fuzzy Inference System*, which is discussed later in this book.

Fuzzy Systems are comprised of Fuzzy Sets and not the normal, classical sets. In these systems, you try to follow Fuzzy Logic, because traditional logic cannot be applied to real-world applications. Let's look at Fuzzy Systems with the help of an example.

When you drive a car, it's a combination of pressing the accelerator and the brake. Whenever you speed up, you press the accelerator, and whenever you want to slow down, you press the brakes. Suppose you are talking about self-driving cars. In this scenario, both systems should be managed simultaneously, without any manual intervention.

If you consider traditional logic, it follows classical sets (called *crisp sets*). In these sets, the value is equal to 0 or 1. Suppose the functioning is defined as shown Table 1-2.

Table 1-2. *Applying Brakes Represented Using Crisp Sets*

Function	Set Code
Press the accelerator	1
Release the accelerator	0
Press the brakes	1
Release the brakes	0

The problem with this encoding is that 1 represents a full pressing and 0 represents a full release. There is no intermediate response. Suppose a car turns in front of your car. In this scenario, the 1 code will get activated and full brakes will be applied. If that car accelerates and is farther away from you, full brakes will be released and the full accelerator will be pressed (codes 0 and 1 will get activated).

Classical Sets

Classical sets, also called *crisp sets*, are a collection of objects. Objects can be anything belonging in the real world, and sometimes outside the domain as well. For example:

```
Cars = {Audi, BMW, Mercedes, Porsche}
```

This set shows a list of premium cars. You denote a set by using the curly braces, {}.

Once you have effectively defined different sets, you can visualize them as well. A *Venn diagram* is a visual way to represent sets and their relationships with each other. Figure 1-2 shows a normal Venn diagram.

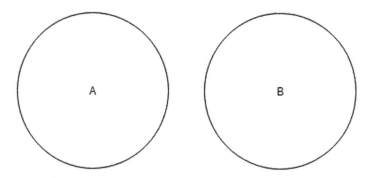

Figure 1-2. *Simple Venn diagram*

The circles in Figure 1-2 represent two sets, A and B. All the elements that are part of Set A will be present in Circle A, while all the elements that are part of Set B will be present in Circle B. The circles are called Venn diagrams of Set A and Set B.

Universe of Discourse

All the possible elements that can share a domain, or have similar characteristics, are contained in a set. The set of those elements is called the *Universe of Discourse*. Once you have this set, you can form various subsets as well. Formally speaking, the Universe of Discourse can be defined as follows:

> *"In every discourse, whether of the mind conversing with its own thoughts, or of the individual in his intercourse with others, there is an assumed or expressed limit within which the subjects of its operation are confined. ... Now, whatever may be the extent of the field within which all the objects of our discourse are found, that field may properly be termed the Universe of Discourse. (Boole 1854/1958, p. 42)"*

Look at the Universe of Discourse with the following example:

$$E = \{Domain\ of\ Machine\ Learning\}$$

Let Set E be the Universe of Discourse. It has the complete domain of Machine Learning. Then the possible sets that can be part of E are:

- Set of Machine Learning algorithms

- Set of basic statistical methods

- Set of neural networks, etc.

Properties of Classical Sets

This section explains the various properties of classical sets. These are:

- Membership of elements

- Cardinality of sets

- Family of sets

- Null set

- Singleton set

- Subset

- Superset

- Powerset

- Countable set

- Uncountable set

Membership of Elements

If an element is a part of a set, it is called a *member* of the set. It is denoted by $X \varepsilon A$, which means that Element X is a member of Set A.

$$A = \{1,2,3,4,5\}$$

In the set of integers from 1 to 5, each number is called a member of Set A.

Cardinality of Sets

In a set, if you count the total number of elements present, that number is called the *cardinality* of the set. It can be denoted by n(A) or |A| or #A.

$$A = \{1,2,3,4,5\}$$

This set has a cardinality of 5.

Family of Sets

A set can contain anything. But if a set contains a collection of different sets, then that set is referred to as a *family* of sets. For example:

$$A = \{(1,3,5),(2,4,6),(5,10,15)\}$$

Here, (1, 3, 5), (2, 4, 6), and (5, 10, 15) are individual sets contained in Set A. Therefore, Set A is the family of sets, as shown in Figure 1-3.

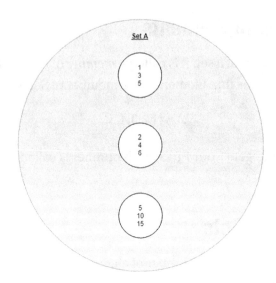

Figure 1-3. *The Family Set A contains different sets*

Null Set

If a set has a cardinality of 0, it's called a *null set* or *empty set*. That means that there are no elements inside it.

A = {} is a null set.

Singleton Set

If a set has a cardinality of 1, it is called a *singleton set*. That means that there is only one element inside it.

A = {1} is a singleton set.

Subset

Say you have two sets, A and X. If all the elements of X are part of A, then X is called a *subset* of A. It is represented by X⊂A. Figure 1-4 shows a Venn diagram representing Superset A containing Subset X.

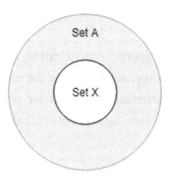

Figure 1-4. *Venn diagram representing Superset A and Subset X*

Superset

Say you have two sets, A and X. If all the elements of X are part of A, then A is called the *superset* of X. It is represented by A⊃X. In the Figure 1-4, A is the superset of X.

Powerset

Say you have a set A. A set containing all the possible subsets from A, including the null set, is called the *powerset.* It is represented by P(A). The cardinality of the powerset of A is 2|A|.

For example:

$$If\ A = \{2010,2011\}$$

$$P(A) = \{(2010),(2011),(2010,2011),(\ )\}$$

As you can see, |A| = 2, while |P(A)| = 4.

Countable Set

A *countable set* is where for every element can be labeled a unique natural number. Also, by the time you finish labeling the elements, more labels are left in the form of natural numbers, or otherwise you have exhausted all the natural numbers. Therefore, infinite sets can also be countable, but not every time.

Uncountable Set

An *uncountable set* is where, for every element present, you cannot label a unique natural number. That means, by the time you finish assigning labels, the natural numbers list is exhausted. For example, when you take real numbers, the list of natural numbers will be exhausted much before the labeling of a set of real numbers is finished.

Classical Set Operations

This section looks at some of the operations that can be applied to classical sets:

- Union
- Intersection
- Complement
- Difference

Union

A *union* of two sets merges the values in both sets into one single set.

$$A = \{1,3,5\}$$

$$B = \{2,4\}$$

$$A \cup B = \{1,2,3,4,5\}$$

Figure 1-5 represents a union between two sets, A and B. The shaded region represents the union part.

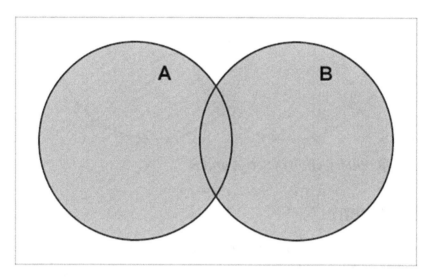

Figure 1-5. *Union of Sets A and B*

Intersection

An *intersection* of two sets finds the common values present in both sets and makes them one single set.

$$A = \{1,3,5\}$$

$$B = \{3\}$$

$$A \cap B = \{3\}$$

Figure 1-6 represents an intersection between two Sets A and B. The shaded region represents the intersection part.

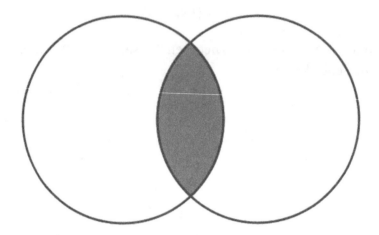

Figure 1-6. *Intersection of Sets A and B*

Complement

A *complement* of a set is all the values present in the Universe of Discourse, except the ones present in the set.

$$A = \{1,3,5\}$$

$$B = \{3\}$$

If A is the Universe of Discourse for B, then A^c will be all the values except the existing one. That is:

$$A^c = \{1,5\}$$

Figure 1-7 represents the complement of Set A. If U is the Universe of Discourse, then the shaded region represents the complement of A.

U

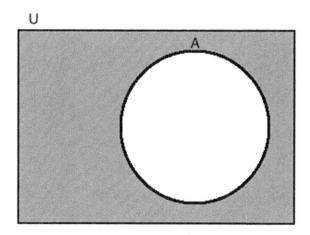

Figure 1-7. *Complement of Set A*

Difference

Say you have two sets, A and B, and you need to find the difference between them. All those values that are not common to both sets become a set. That means that the difference between Sets A and B becomes the set of elements. That set contains elements only in A but not in B.

$$A = \{1,3,5\}$$

$$B = \{3\}$$

$$A - B = \{1,5\}$$

$$B - A = \{\ \}$$

Figure 1-8 shows a Venn diagram representing the difference between Sets A and B.

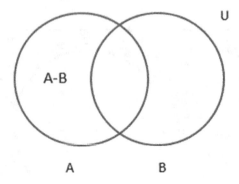

Figure 1-8. *Difference between Sets A and B*

Here's the Python implementation:

```
# Example Sets
A = {0, 2, 4, 6, 8}
B = {1, 2, 3, 4, 5}

# union of above sets
print("Union :", A | B)

# intersection of above sets
print("Intersection :", A & B)

# difference between above sets
print("Difference :", A - B)
```

Crisp Set Properties

This section discusses the following properties of classical/crisp sets:

- Law of Commutativity

- Law of Associativity

- Law of Distributivity

- Idempotent Law

- Identity Law

- Law of Absorption

- Involution Law

- Law of Transitivity

- Law of Excluded Middle

- Law of Contradiction

- De Morgan laws

Law of Commutativity

The union or intersection of two sets will produce the same the result, regardless of which set you list first. That means you can take A first or B first, but the results will always be the same.

$$(A \cup B) = (B \cup A)$$

$$(A \cap B) = (B \cap A)$$

Law of Associativity

If you have three sets, the Law of Associativity says that a union or intersection of the first two sets with the third one is equal to a union or intersection of the last two sets with the first one.

$$(A \cup B) \cup C = A \cup (B \cup C)$$

$$(A \cap B) \cap C = A \cap (B \cap C)$$

Law of Distributivity

The Law of Distributivity says that a union of the first set with an intersection of the last two sets is equal to a union of the first set with the second, a union of the first set with the third, and then an intersection of both outputs. This same rule applies when you interchange the union and intersection operations.

$$A \cup (B \cap C) = (A \cup B) \cap (A \cup C)$$

$$A \cap (B \cup C) = (A \cap B) \cup (A \cap C)$$

Idempotent Law

The Idempotent Law states that an intersection or union of a set with the same set is the same set itself.

$$A \cup A = A$$

$$A \cap A = A$$

Identity Law

If Φ is an empty set and E is a Universe of Discourse, then the Identity Law states that:

$$A \cup \Phi = A$$

$$A \cup E = E$$

$$A \cap \Phi = \Phi$$

$$A \cap E = A$$

In other words:

- A union of a set with an empty set leads to the same set

- An intersection of a set with an empty set leads to an empty set

- A union of a set with a Universe of Discourse leads to the Union of Discourse

- An intersection of a set with a Universe of Discourse leads to the same set

Law of Absorption

If A is a subset of B, then:

$$A \cup (A \cap B) = A$$

$$A \cap (A \cup B) = A$$

This means that the union of a set with its intersection with another set is the same set, and vice versa.

Involution Law

The Involution Law states that the double complement of a set is the same set:

$$(A^c)^c = A$$

Law of Transitivity

The Law of Transitivity states that if A is a subset of B and B is a subset of C, then A will be a subset of C.

$$If\ A \subseteq B, B \subseteq C, then\ A \subseteq C$$

Law of Excluded Middle

The Law of Excluded Middle states that a union of a set with its complement is its Universe of Discourse.

$$\left(A \cup A^c \right) = E$$

Law of Contradiction

The Law of Contradiction states that an intersection of a set with its complement is an empty set.

$$\left(A \cap A^c \right) = \Phi$$

De Morgan Laws

If there are two sets and you find the complement of the union between them, then it is equal to the intersection of the complements of the individual sets. Similarly, if you find the complement of the intersection between the two sets, it is equal to the union of the complements of the individual sets. This rule is called the De Morgan Laws.

$$\left(A \cup B \right)^c = A^c \cap B^c$$

$$\left(A \cap B \right)^c = A^c \cup B^c$$

Fuzzy Sets

Classical sets involve exactly defined values. This means that the Universe of Discourse is split into two groups—members and non-members. Therefore, you cannot say that any member has a partial membership. For example, if you are pressing brakes or releasing them, these processes can be represented by 1 or 0.

With Fuzzy Sets, on the other hand, you can have values in between as well. Therefore, you can say that the Fuzzy Sets have a degree of membership between 0 and 1. For example, you can have values like {0, 0.3, 0.5, 0.7, 1}. The 1 means a full brake, 0.7 means a little less brake, 0.5 means half the pressure, 0.3 means very little pressure, and 0 means no pressure. In the real world, you rarely see classical sets in action. You deal with the values represented by Fuzzy Sets.

There are several properties associated with Fuzzy Sets. The next sections explain them:

- Law of Commutativity
- Law of Associativity
- Law of Distributivity
- Idempotent Law
- Identity Law
- Involution Law
- Law of Transitivity
- De Morgan laws

Law of Commutativity

The union or intersection of two sets produces the same the result, regardless of which set you list first. That means you can take A first or B first, but the results will always be the same.

$$(A \cup B) = (B \cup A)$$

$$(A \cap B) = (B \cap A)$$

Law of Associativity

Say you have three sets. The Law of Associativity says that a union or intersection of the first two sets with the third one is equal to a union or intersection of the last two sets with the first one.

$$(A \cup B) \cup C = A \cup (B \cup C)$$

$$(A \cap B) \cap C = A \cap (B \cap C)$$

Law of Distributivity

The Law of Distributivity says that a union of the first set with an intersection of the last two sets is equal to a union of the first set with the second, a union of the first set with the third, and then an intersection of both outputs. This same rule applies when you interchange the union and intersection operations.

$$A \cup (B \cap C) = (A \cup B) \cap (A \cup C)$$

$$A \cap (B \cup C) = (A \cap B) \cup (A \cap C)$$

Idempotent Law

The Idempotent Law states that an intersection or union of a set with the same set is the same set itself.

$$A \cup A = A$$

$$A \cap A = A$$

Identity Law

If Φ is an empty set and E is a universe of discourse, the Identity Law states that:

$$A \cup \Phi = A$$

$$A \cup E = E$$

$$A \cap \Phi = \Phi$$

$$A \cap E = A$$

In other words:

- A union of a set with an empty set leads to the same set
- An intersection of a set with an empty set leads to an empty set
- A union of a set with a Universe of Discourse leads to a Union of Discourse
- An intersection of a set with a Universe of Discourse leads to the same set

Involution Law

The Involution Law states that a double complement of a set leads to the same set:

$$(A^c)^c = A$$

Law of Transitivity

The Law of Transitivity states that if A is a subset of B and B is a subset of C, A will be a subset of C.

$$If\ A \subseteq B,\ B \subseteq C,\ then\ A \subseteq C$$

De Morgan Laws

If there are two sets and you find the complement of the union between them, it is equal to the intersection of the complements of the individual sets. Similarly, if you find the complement of an intersection between the two sets, it is equal to the union of the complements of the individual sets. This rule is called De Morgan Laws.

$$\left(A \cup B\right)^c = A^c \cap B^c$$

$$\left(A \cap B\right)^c = A^c \cup B^c$$

Now, before you learn about the operations that can be applied to Fuzzy Sets, you need to understand the concept of membership functions.

Introduction to Membership Functions

In the previous section, you learned that instead of having crisp values of 0 and 1, each element can be mapped to a value between 0 and 1. Each value is called the *degree* of membership and is represented by a curve, which depicts a function called a *membership function*. The value is called the *membership value*. In Figure 1-9, you can see the difference between crisp and Fuzzy Sets.

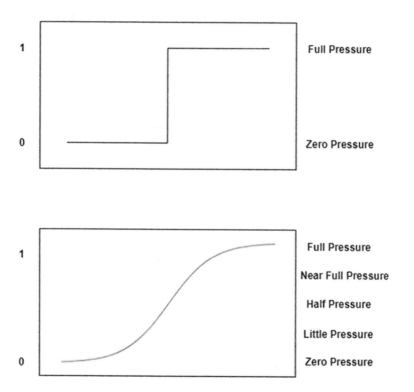

Figure 1-9. *Difference between Fuzzy and crisp set representations*

In a crisp set, you only have two values, represented by 0 and 1, but in a Fuzzy Set, there is a range of values, based on the pressure at which the breaks are applied. The curve representing the range is the membership function curve. With a different pressure, a different membership value will be present, and that can be represented in the membership function curve.

Let's look at the membership function and its related concepts in a little more depth.

A Fuzzy Set is an extension and gross oversimplification of a classical set. If X is the Universe of Discourse and its elements are denoted by x, then a Fuzzy Set A in X is defined as a set of ordered pairs.

$$A = \{x, \mu A(x) | x \varepsilon X\}$$

$\mu_A(x)$ is called the membership function of x in A. The membership function maps each element of X to a membership value between 0 and 1. There are different types of membership functions, which are covered in detail in the next chapter. For now, let's list some of them and look at the curves that they represent. This example uses the Scikit Fuzzy package, which has multiple methods and classes, so that you can apply the basic Fuzzy Operations effectively. You can use the following line to install the Scikit Fuzzy package in the Python environment:

pip install scikit − fuzzy

Figures 1-10 through 1-14 show the different types of membership functions and the curves that they represent.

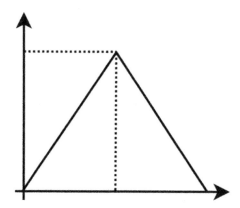

Figure 1-10. *Triangular membership function*

The graph in Figure 1-10 represents a triangular membership function, and you can use the `trimf` method from the `skfuzzy` package to find and plot the points.

Here is the sample code. The next chapter discusses this function in detail.

The following code takes an example where a person goes into a restaurant and tips a waiter. For tipping purposes, the quality of service is rated from 0 to 10. This example looks only at the service quality for now, but later it will discuss the actual tipping problem.

```
import numpy as np
import skfuzzy as sk

#Defining the Numpy array for Tip Quality
x_qual = np.arange(0, 11, 1)

#Defining the Numpy array for Triangular membership functions
qual_lo = sk.trimf(x_qual, [0, 0, 5])
```

The graph in Figure 1-11 represents a trapezoidal membership function, and you can use the `trapmf` method from the `skfuzzy` package to find and plot the points.

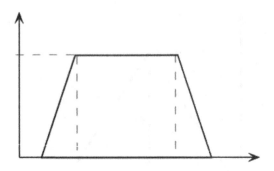

Figure 1-11. *Trapezoidal membership function*

Here is the sample code.

```
import numpy as np
import skfuzzy as sk

#Defining the Numpy array for Tip Quality
x_qual = np.arange(0, 11, 1)

#Defining the Numpy array for Trapezoidal membership functions
qual_lo = sk.trapmf(x_qual, [0, 0, 5,5])
```

The graph in Figure 1-12 represents a Gaussian membership function, and you can use the gaussmf method from the skfuzzy package to find and plot the points.

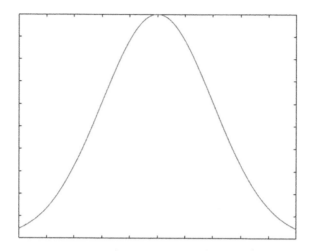

Figure 1-12. *Gaussian membership function*

Here is the sample code.

```
import numpy as np
import skfuzzy as sk

#Defining the Numpy array for Tip Quality
x_qual = np.arange(0, 11, 1)

#Defining the Numpy array for Gaussian membership functions
qual_lo = sk.gaussmf(x_qual, np.mean(x_qual), np.std(x_qual))
```

The graph in Figure 1-13 represents a generalized bell membership function, and you can use the gbellmf method from the skfuzzy package to find and plot the points.

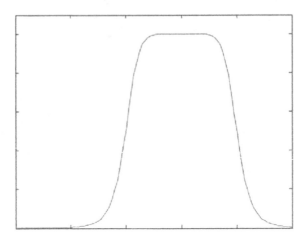

Figure 1-13. *Generalized bell membership function*

Here is the sample code.

```
import numpy as np
import skfuzzy as sk

#Defining the Numpy array for Tip Quality
x_qual = np.arange(0, 11, 1)

#Defining the Numpy array for Generalized Bell membership
functions
qual_lo = sk.gbellmf(x_qual, 0.5, 0.5, 0.5)
```

The graph in Figure 1-14 represents a sigmoidal membership function, and you can use the sigmf method from the skfuzzy package to find and plot the points.

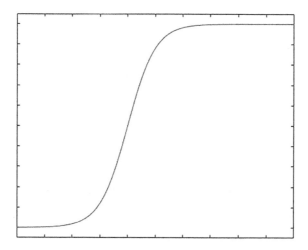

Figure 1-14. *Sigmoidal membership function*

Here is the sample code.

```
import numpy as np
import skfuzzy as sk

#Defining the Numpy array for Tip Quality
x_qual = np.arange(0, 11, 1)

#Defining the Numpy array for Sigmoid membership functions
qual_lo = sk.sigmf(x_qual, 0.5,0.5)
```

Later chapters cover all these functions in greater detail.

Fuzzy Set Operations

Now that you have learned about the concept of membership functions, it's time to look at some of the operations that can be done with Fuzzy Sets. This section discusses the following operations:

- Union

- Intersection

- Complement

- Product

- Equality

- Power

- Difference

- Disjunctive sum

Suppose there are two Fuzzy Sets, A and B, having a membership value as $\mu_A(x)$ and $\mu_B(x)$, where X is the Universe of Discourse. Based on this information, the following sections consider each operation in detail.

Union

The union of two Fuzzy Sets A and B is a new Fuzzy Set, A ∪ B, also on X with a membership function defined as follows:

$$\mu_{(A\cup B)} = max\big(\mu_A(x),\mu_B(x)\big) = \mu_A(x)\wedge\mu_B(x)$$

∧ is called the *maximum operator*.

Here is the Python implementation:

```
import skfuzzy as sk
import numpy as np

#Defining the Numpy array for Tip Quality
x_qual = np.arange(0, 11, 1)

#Defining the Numpy array for two membership functions (Triangular)
qual_lo = sk.trimf(x_qual, [0, 0, 5])
qual_md = sk.trimf(x_qual, [0, 5, 10])

#Finding the Maximum (Fuzzy Or)
sk.fuzzy_or(x_qual,qual_lo,x_qual,qual_hi)
```

Intersection

An intersection of Fuzzy Sets A and B is a new Fuzzy Set, A ∩ B, also on X whose membership function is defined by:

$$\mu_{(A \cap B)} = min\left(\mu_A(x), \mu_B(x)\right) = \mu_A(x) \vee \mu_B(x)$$

is called the minimum operator.

Here is the Python implementation:

```
import skfuzzy as sk
import numpy as np

#Defining the Numpy array for Tip Quality
x_qual = np.arange(0, 11, 1)

#Defining the Numpy array for two membership functions
(Triangular)
qual_lo = sk.trimf(x_qual, [0, 0, 5])
qual_md = sk.trimf(x_qual, [0, 5, 10])

#Finding the Minimum (Fuzzy AND)
sk.fuzzy_and(x_qual,qual_lo,x_qual,qual_hi)
```

Complement

The complement of a Fuzzy Set A is A with this membership function:

$$\mu_{\bar{A}}(x) = 1 - \mu_A(x)$$

Here is the Python implementation:

```
import skfuzzy as sk
import numpy as np
```

```
#Defining the Numpy array for Tip Quality
x_qual = np.arange(0, 11, 1)
```

```
#Defining the Numpy array for two membership functions (Triangular)
qual_lo = sk.trimf(x_qual, [0, 0, 5])
qual_md = sk.trimf(x_qual, [0, 5, 10])
```

```
#Finding the Complement (Fuzzy NOT)
sk.fuzzy_not(qual_lo)
```

Product

The product of two Fuzzy Sets A and B is a new Fuzzy Set, A.B, with this membership function:

$$\mu_{A.B}(x) = \mu_A(x) \cdot \mu_B(x)$$

Here is the Python implementation:

```
import skfuzzy as sk
import numpy as np
```

```
#Defining the Numpy array for Tip Quality
x_qual = np.arange(0, 11, 1)
```

```
#Defining the Numpy array for two membership functions
(Triangular)
qual_lo = sk.trimf(x_qual, [0, 0, 5])
qual_md = sk.trimf(x_qual, [0, 5, 10])
```

```
#Finding the Product (Fuzzy Cartesian)
sk.cartprod(qual_lo, qual_hi)
```

Difference

The difference of two Fuzzy Sets A and B is a new Fuzzy Set, A-B, which is defined as

$$A - B = \left(A \cap \overline{B} \right)$$

Here is the Python implementation:

```
import skfuzzy as sk
import numpy as np

#Defining the Numpy array for Tip Quality
x_qual = np.arange(0, 11, 1)

#Defining the Numpy array for two membership functions
(Triangular)
qual_lo = sk.trimf(x_qual, [0, 0, 5])
qual_md = sk.trimf(x_qual, [0, 5, 10])

#Finding the Difference (Fuzzy Subtract)
sk.fuzzy_sub(x_qual,qual_lo,x_qual,qual_hi)
```

Disjunctive Sum

The disjunctive sum is the new Fuzzy Set defined as follows:

$$A \oplus B = \left(\overline{A} \cap B \right) \cup \left(A \cap \overline{B} \right)$$

Power

The alpha power of a Fuzzy Set A is a new Fuzzy Set Aα, whose membership function is as follows:

$$\mu_A^{\alpha}(x) = \left[\mu_A(x)\right]^{\alpha}$$

Summary

This chapter discussed the classical/crisp sets and Fuzzy Sets. You looked at the differences between them and their properties. You also looked at some of the operations that can be performed on Fuzzy Sets, as well as the Python implementation. To understand these operations, you read about the basics of membership functions.

The next chapter discusses Fuzzy Logic in detail and explains membership functions with their applications.

CHAPTER 2

Fuzzy Rules and Reasoning

The previous chapter discussed different kinds of sets as well as their properties and operations that can be performed on them. You also looked at some of the operations and their applications in Python. That chapter concluded with a small introduction to the different types of membership functions and their Python applications.

This chapter discusses the membership functions and their applications in detail. You will be looking at their diverse properties and operations. After understanding their roles, you will move on to Fuzzy Relations. You will learn what a Fuzzy Relation is and the properties that influence it.

After you have all the basic understanding required, you will finally move on to Fuzzy Rules and Reasoning, the core of Fuzzy Logic. You will learn about the different kinds of rules and how they are applicable. You will learn how to combine different kinds of rules, which will constitute Fuzzy Reasoning. You will see applications of these concepts in Python as well.

Membership Functions

Membership functions represent the degree of truth of a member in a defined Fuzzy Set. They are curves that define how each point in the input space is mapped to a degree of membership lying between 0 and 1. You may understand this better with the help of an example.

© Himanshu Singh, Yunis Ahmad Lone 2020
H. Singh and Y. A. Lone, *Deep Neuro-Fuzzy Systems with Python*,
https://doi.org/10.1007/978-1-4842-5361-8_2

Suppose you want to rate the service of a particular restaurant. You might rate the service in the following ways:

- Awesome

- Average

- Worst

In classical sets, this can be represented as follows:

$$X = \{'Awesome','Average','Worst\}$$

This can be coded and represented as $X = \{\}$, where 2 represents *Awesome*, 1 represents *Average*, and 0 represents *Worst*.

But you might not want to rate the restaurant in only these three ways. You need different ways for customers to express their sentiments. Therefore, you could add these ratings as well:

- Awesome

- Nice

- Good

- Average

- OK

- Poor

- Worst

If you again use a classical set, it will contain a lot of code. Instead, you can define a function wherein each rating has a specific value. This function will allow you to go beyond the ratings. This function has an upper limit and a lower limit. Consider, for example, the sigmoid function (You learn about all the membership functions in detail, later in this chapter.) The sigmoid function has an upper limit of 1 and a lower limit of 0. That means that all the rating categories will have a value that will fall at a point on that curve (see Figure 2-1).

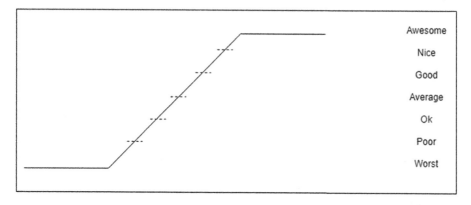

Figure 2-1. *Curve showing all the rating points as specific values*

Looking at this curve, you can redefine the crisp set as a Fuzzy Set having values between 0 and 1. Now, if a person gives a rating, the value (membership value) of that rating can be retrieved from the curve. This is what is meant when we say that membership functions represent the degree of truth of a member. You can see in this example that every rating has a value that tells about its degree of truth.

Formal Definition of a Membership Function

You can write a formal definition of all the rating examples using Fuzzy Notations.

Suppose you have Fuzzy Set A with three members:

$$A = \{x1, x2, x3\}$$

All three members will have a membership function value associated with them, which will define their degree of truth. It can be represented as shown here:

$$A = \left\{ (x1, \mu A(x1)), (x2, \mu A(x2)), (x3, \mu A(x3)) \vee x1, x2, x3 \in X \right\}$$

The higher the membership value, the higher the degree of belonging or truth inside the set. This process where every member of the Fuzzy Set gets a membership value associated with it is called *Fuzzification*. You can now extend the formal notation of the membership function value.

If $\mu_A(x)$ is the membership value of elements and if $\mu_A(x)$ is equal to 1, you say that x is totally present in the Fuzzy Set A, or it has a full membership. If $\mu_A(x)$ is equal to 0, it is not part of A or it has no membership. Any value between 0 and 1 defines its membership, which can be termed part of the membership.

Terminology Related to Fuzzy Membership Functions

To understand Fuzzy Membership Functions in more detail, you must first understand some terminology related to them. This list of terminology will help you understand applications of membership functions better.

- Support
- Core
- Boundary
- Crossover
- Normality
- Fuzzy Singleton
- α- cut

- Strong α- cut

- Convexity

- Bandwidth

- Symmetry

- Open Left

- Open Right

- Closed

Support

The support of a membership function for a Fuzzy Set is defined as that region of the universe that is characterized by nonzero membership in Set A. It is a set of all the points whose membership value is greater than 0, as represented in Figure 2-2. Mathematically, it can be represented as follows:

$$Support(A) = \{(x, \mu A(x)) \vee \mu A(x) > 0\}$$

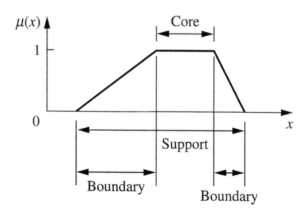

Figure 2-2. *Support, core, and boundary*

Core

The core of a membership function for a Fuzzy Set is defined as that region of the universe that is characterized by complete and full membership in Set A. It is a set of all the points whose membership value is equal to 1, as represented in Figure 2-2. Mathematically, it can be represented as:

$$Core(A) = \{(x, \mu A(x)) \vee \mu A(x) = 1\}$$

Boundary

The boundaries of a membership function for a Fuzzy Set are defined as that region of the universe containing elements that have a nonzero membership but not complete membership. It is a set of all the points whose membership value is greater than 0, but less than 1, as represented in Figure 2-2. Mathematically, it can be represented as follows:

$$0 < \mu_A(x) < 1$$

Crossover

The crossover points of a membership function are defined as the elements in the universe for which a Fuzzy Set has values equal to 0.5. A set of all the points whose membership value is equal to 0.5 is called the crossover of Fuzzy Set A:

$$Crossover(A) = \{(x, \mu A(x)) \vee \mu A(x) = 0.5\}$$

Normality

A normal Fuzzy Set is one whose membership function has at least one element x in the universe whose membership value is unity (see Figure 2-3). In other words, if you find the core of a set and it's not an empty set, you say that the Fuzzy Set A is normal:

$$if, Core(A) \neq \varnothing \rightarrow AisNormal$$

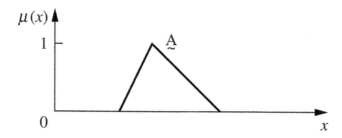

Figure 2-3. *Normality of a Fuzzy Set*

Fuzzy Singleton

If a Fuzzy Set has only one single point, having a membership value of 1, it is called a Fuzzy Singleton:

$$|A| = \left|\left\{(x, \mu A(x)) \vee \mu A(x) = 1\right\}\right|$$

α– Cut

An alpha cut of Fuzzy Set A is a set containing all the values with membership values greater than or equal to alpha:

$$A\alpha = \left\{x \in X \vee \mu A(x) \geq \alpha\right\}$$

Strong $\alpha-$ Cut

A string alpha cut of Fuzzy Set A is a set containing all the values having membership values greater than alpha:

$$A\alpha = \left\{x \in X \vee \mu A(x) > \alpha\right\}$$

Convexity

A convex Fuzzy Set is described by a membership function whose membership values are strictly monotonically increasing, or whose membership values are strictly monotonically decreasing, or whose membership values are strictly monotonically increasing and then strictly monotonically decreasing, with increasing values for elements in the universe. In simpler terms, a Fuzzy Set is called convex if and only if it follows this rule:

$$\mu_A\left(\lambda x + (1-\lambda)y\right) \geq \min\left\{\mu_A(x), \mu_A(y)\right\}$$

Bandwidth

If you have a set A, which is normal and convex, and if you find its crossover set and select two unique points, the distance between the two is called the bandwidth set. Simply speaking, for a normal and convex Fuzzy Set, the bandwidth is defined as the distance between the two unique crossover points:

$$Bandwidth(A) = |x2 - x1| \rightarrow \mu_A(x1) = \mu_A(x2) = 0.5$$

Symmetry

If the membership function of a Fuzzy Set A satisfies the following criteria, at a point c, it is called a symmetric set (see Figure 2-4).

$$\mu_A(x+c) = \mu_A(c-x) \forall x \in X$$

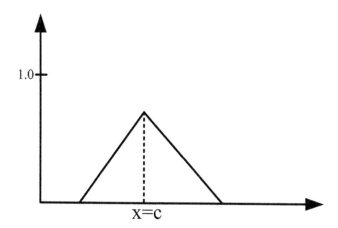

Figure 2-4. *Symmetry of Fuzzy Set*

Open Left

A Fuzzy Set is open left if (see Figure 2-5):

$$A \Leftrightarrow \mu_A(x) = 1 \wedge \mu_A(x) = 0$$

Open Right

A Fuzzy Set is open right if (see Figure 2-5):

$$A \Leftrightarrow \mu_A(x) = 0 \wedge \mu_A(x) = 1$$

Closed

A Fuzzy Set is closed if (see Figure 2-5):

$$A \Leftrightarrow \mu_A(x) = \mu_A(x) = 0$$

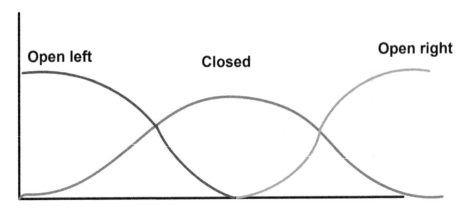

Figure 2-5. *Open Left, closed, and open right sets*

Types of Membership Functions

The first chapter covered the different types of membership functions in brief. This section discusses them in detail. A membership function is used to define Fuzziness present in a problem statement. This means that you don't have to represent all the values in a sample space using discrete numbers. Sometimes a member can be a decimal representing its degree of membership.

For example, consider the penalty kick concept in soccer. In discrete terms, the kick can be either 1 (a full kick) or 0 (no kick). In real life, that is not the case. The kick speed depends not only on the mindset of the shooter, but also on the anticipation of where the goalkeeper will move.

In this situation, the shooter decides the speed of the kick as well as the direction in which he aims. Speed also cannot be defined just by two discrete values, 0 and 1. The speed will range from 0 to 1; 0 being no speed and 1 being full speed. Suppose the shooter wants to aim for the top-right corner of the goal post. In this situation, the major decision is finding the most accurate speed that can give the ball a perfect swing. Too fast and the ball will leave the post, while too slow might help the goalkeeper anticipate the direction or prevent the ball from swinging properly. Hence, instead of going for 1, the shooter may go for 0.7 from a Fuzzy Set, which according to him is the ideal speed to kick the ball. This concept in a Fuzzy Set is represented by the membership functions.

The next section discusses the different types of membership functions that are used.

Triangular Membership Function

Just as a triangle has three coordinates, a triangular membership function has three parameters: a, b, and c.

- a is the lower boundary

- b is the center

- c is the upper boundary

The following equation depicts the triangular membership function:

$$f(x; a, b, c) = \begin{cases} 0, & x \le a \\ \dfrac{x-a}{b-a}, & a \le x \le b \\ \dfrac{c-x}{c-b}, & b \le x \le c \\ 0, & c \le x \end{cases}$$

Alternatively, this can also be represented as follows:

$$f(x; a, b, c) = \max\left(\min\left(\frac{x-a}{b-a}, \frac{c-x}{c-b} \right), 0 \right)$$

You can understand the triangular membership functions with the help of an example. This example uses the triangular membership function with a soccer example. Suppose the shooter can take four kinds of penalty shots:

- Full speed straight shot

- Medium powered curvy shot

45

- Slow straight shot

- Medium fast left shot

On average, the top speed at which a shooter takes a penalty kick is 80 mph. Therefore, there is no way you can say that this speed is slow. Hence you assign a 0% membership to 80mph. Similarly, a speed of 60 mph can be considered 70% fast and 30% medium. Likewise, you can assign different memberships to different speeds.

If you use a triangular membership function, it contains three limits: lower, full, and upper. The lower and upper bounds have a membership of 0% while the full value is 100%. The remaining values tread linearly. You can assign the following triangular membership functions to these categories:

- Full speed as [60, 80, 80]

- Medium powered as [40, 50, 70]

- Slow as [20, 20, 45]

- Medium fast as [50, 60, 80]

For example, if you defined the triangular membership function for "medium powered" as [40, 50, 70], the membership would be 0% at 40 mph, which linearly increases to 100% at 50 mph, and linearly decreases to 0% at 70 mph. The following Python code shows the execution of these triangular membership functions. Figure 2-6 shows the result.

```
#Importing Necessary Packages
import numpy as np
import skfuzzy as fuzz
import matplotlib.pyplot as plt
%matplotlib inline

#Defining the Fuzzy Range from a speed of 30 to 90
x = np.arange(30, 80, 0.1)
```

```
#Defining the triangular membership functions
slow = fuzz.trimf(x, [30, 30, 50])
medium = fuzz.trimf(x, [30, 50, 70])
medium_fast = fuzz.trimf(x, [50, 60, 80])
full_speed = fuzz.trimf(x, [60, 80, 80])

#Plotting the Membership Functions Defined
plt.figure()
plt.plot(x, full_speed, 'b', linewidth=1.5, label='Full Speed')
plt.plot(x, medium_fast, 'k', linewidth=1.5, label='Medium Fast')
plt.plot(x, medium, 'm', linewidth=1.5, label='Medium Powered')
plt.plot(x, slow, 'r', linewidth=1.5, label='Slow')
plt.title('Penalty Kick Fuzzy')
plt.ylabel('Membership')
plt.xlabel("Speed (Miles Per Hour)")
plt.legend(loc='center right', bbox_to_anchor=(1.25, 0.5),
ncol=1, fancybox=True, shadow=True)
```

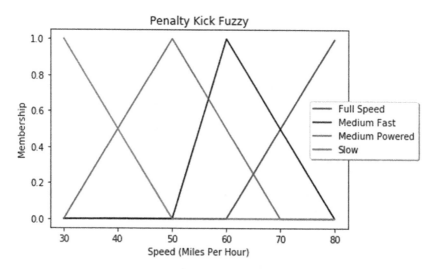

Figure 2-6. *Triangular membership of the soccer example*

Trapezoidal Membership Function

A trapezoid has four coordinates, so the membership function also has four coordinates values: a, b, c, and d, for a crisp value x. However, keep in mind this rule:

$$b < c < d$$

You can describe the function using this equation:

$$f(x; a, b, c, d) = \max\left(\min\left(\frac{x-a}{b-a}, 1, \frac{d-x}{d-c} \right), o \right)$$

This equation can be expanded with multiple cut-points:

$$f(x; a, b, c, d) = \begin{cases} 0, & x \leq a \\ \dfrac{x-a}{b-a}, & a \leq x \leq b \\ 1, & b \leq x \leq c \\ \dfrac{d-x}{d-c}, & c \leq x \leq d \\ 0, & d \leq x \end{cases}$$

In trapezoidal membership functions, you need to provide four points. With the soccer example, you have to provide a range based on a specific class. In this membership function, the membership reaches 100% from 0% in the center, and then again drops to 0%. Instead of three points, as with the triangular membership function, you have four points. This applies the soccer example to the trapezoidal membership function, whose classes are defined as follows:

- Full speed as [60, 80, 80, 90]

- Medium powered as [30, 50, 50, 70]

- Slow as [20, 30, 30, 50]

- Medium fast as [50, 60, 60, 80])

Here is the Python implementation; the result is shown in Figure 2-7.

```python
#Importing Necessary Packages
import numpy as np
import skfuzzy as fuzz
import matplotlib.pyplot as plt
%matplotlib inline

#Defining the Fuzzy Range from a speed of 30 to 90
x = np.arange(30, 90, 0.1)

#Defining the trapezoidal membership functions
slow = fuzz.trapmf(x, [20, 30, 30, 50])
medium = fuzz.trapmf(x, [30, 50, 50, 70])
medium_fast = fuzz.trapmf(x, [50, 60, 60, 80])
full_speed = fuzz.trapmf(x, [60, 80, 80, 90])

#Plotting the Membership Functions Defined
plt.figure()
plt.plot(x, full_speed, 'b', linewidth=1.5, label='Full Speed')
plt.plot(x, medium_fast, 'k', linewidth=1.5, label='Medium Fast')
plt.plot(x, medium, 'm', linewidth=1.5, label='Medium Powered')
plt.plot(x, slow, 'r', linewidth=1.5, label='Slow')
plt.title('Penalty Kick Fuzzy')
plt.ylabel('Membership')
plt.xlabel("Speed (Miles Per Hour)")
plt.legend(loc='center right', bbox_to_anchor=(1.25, 0.5),
ncol=1, fancybox=True, shadow=True)
```

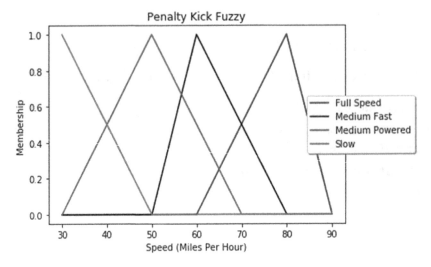

Figure 2-7. *Trapezoidal membership of the soccer example*

Gaussian Membership Function

When you know the mean and standard deviation of the crisp values and want to take into consideration the customizable Fuzzification Factor as well, you use Gaussian membership functions. They can be represented using the equation:

$$\mu_A(x,c,s,m) = e^{\frac{-1}{2}\left|\frac{x-c}{s}\right|^m}$$

where c and s are the mean and standard deviation, respectively, and m is the Fuzzification Factor.

When you apply the Gaussian membership function to the soccer example, you can see that the values are represented much better and the interpolation is smooth. You define the Gaussian membership of the classes as follows:

- Full speed has a mean of 80 mph and a standard deviation of 4

- Medium powered has a mean of 50 mph and a standard deviation of 4

- Slow has a mean of 30 mph and a standard deviation of 4

- Medium fast has a mean of 60 mph and a standard deviation of 4

You can always play with the standard deviation. Here is the Python implementation of the soccer example using the Gaussian membership function. Figure 2-8 shows the result.

```
#Importing Necessary Packages
import numpy as np
import skfuzzy as fuzz
import matplotlib.pyplot as plt
%matplotlib inline

#Defining the Fuzzy Range from a speed of 30 to 90
x = np.arange(30, 90, 0.1)

#Defining the gaussian membership functions
full_speed = fuzz.gaussmf(x, 80, 4)
medium_fast = fuzz.gaussmf(x, 60, 4)
medium = fuzz.gaussmf(x, 50, 4)
slow = fuzz.gaussmf(x, 30, 4)

#Plotting the Membership Functions Defined
plt.figure()
plt.plot(x, full_speed, 'b', linewidth=1.5, label='Full Speed')
plt.plot(x, medium_fast, 'k', linewidth=1.5, label='Medium Fast')
plt.plot(x, medium, 'm', linewidth=1.5, label='Medium Powered')
plt.plot(x, slow, 'r', linewidth=1.5, label='Slow')
plt.title('Penalty Kick Fuzzy')
plt.ylabel('Membership')
```

```
plt.xlabel("Speed (Miles Per Hour)")
plt.legend(loc='center right', bbox_to_anchor=(1.25, 0.5),
ncol=1, fancybox=True, shadow=True)
```

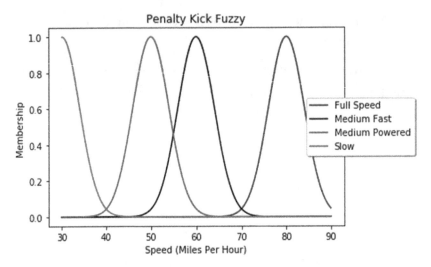

Figure 2-8. *Gaussian membership of the soccer example*

Generalized Bell Membership Function

The generalized bell membership function takes into consideration three parameters:

- The slope

- The center

- The width of the curve

It is represented by the following equation:

$$gbell(x,a,b,c) = \frac{1}{1+\left|\dfrac{x-c}{b}\right|^{2b}}$$

where a represents the width, b represents the slope, and c represents the center.

If you solve the soccer example with the generalized bell function, you'll get the following membership functions:

- Full speed has a center at 80 mph while the width and slope are 8 and 4, respectively

- Medium powered has a center at 50 mph while the width and slope are 8 and 4, respectively

- Slow has a center at 30 mph while the width and slope are 8 and 4, respectively

- Medium fast has a center at 60 mph while the width and slope are 8 and 4, respectively

```
#Importing Necessary Packages
import numpy as np
import skfuzzy as fuzz
import matplotlib.pyplot as plt
%matplotlib inline

#Defining the Fuzzy Range from a speed of 30 to 90
x = np.arange(30, 90, 0.1)

#Defining the generalized bell membership functions
full_speed = fuzz.gbellmf(x, 8,4,80)
medium_fast = fuzz.gbellmf(x, 8,4,60)
medium = fuzz.gbellmf(x, 8,4,50)
slow = fuzz.gbellmf(x, 8,4,30)

#Plotting the Membership Functions Defined
plt.figure()
plt.plot(x, full_speed, 'b', linewidth=1.5, label='Full Speed')
plt.plot(x, medium_fast, 'k', linewidth=1.5, label='Medium Fast')
```

```
plt.plot(x, medium, 'm', linewidth=1.5, label='Medium Powered')
plt.plot(x, slow, 'r', linewidth=1.5, label='Slow')
plt.title('Penalty Kick Fuzzy')
plt.ylabel('Membership')
plt.xlabel("Speed (Miles Per Hour)")
plt.legend(loc='center right', bbox_to_anchor=(1.25, 0.5),
ncol=1, fancybox=True, shadow=True)
```

Figure 2-9 shows the result.

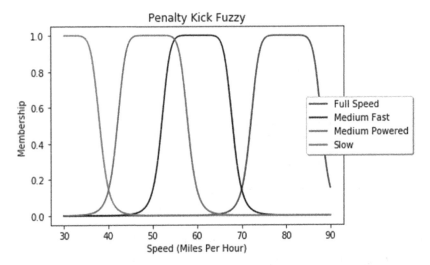

Figure 2-9. *Generalized bell membership of the soccer example*

Sigmoidal Membership Function

This is one of the most widely used membership functions, especially in the field of neural networks. The formula is given here:

$$Sigmoid(x; a, c) = \frac{1}{1 + e^{-a(x-c)}}$$

where a represents the slope and c represents the crossover point.

When you come to a specific instance wherein you must take care of very high values or very low values, you use the sigmoidal membership function as the target.

You must provide two points, and the most important point is the c point (crossover point), which represents the center. Therefore, for the soccer example, the classes will be redefined using the sigmoidal membership function as follows:

- Full speed has a crossover at 80 mph and a slope of 2

- Medium powered has a crossover at 50 mph and a slope of 2

- Slow has a crossover at 30 mph and a slope of 2

- Medium fast has a crossover at 60 mph and a slope of 2

Here is the Python implementation.

```python
#Importing Necessary Packages
import numpy as np
import skfuzzy as fuzz
import matplotlib.pyplot as plt
%matplotlib inline

#Defining the Fuzzy Range from a speed of 30 to 90
x = np.arange(30, 90, 0.1)

#Defining the sigmoidal membership functions
full_speed = fuzz.sigmf(x, 80,2)
medium_fast = fuzz.sigmf(x, 60,2)
medium = fuzz.sigmf(x, 50,2)
slow = fuzz.sigmf(x, 30,2)

#Plotting the Membership Functions Defined
plt.figure()
plt.plot(x, full_speed, 'b', linewidth=1.5, label='Full Speed')
```

```
plt.plot(x, medium_fast, 'k', linewidth=1.5, label='Medium Fast')
plt.plot(x, medium, 'm', linewidth=1.5, label='Medium Powered')
plt.plot(x, slow, 'r', linewidth=1.5, label='Slow')
plt.title('Penalty Kick Fuzzy')
plt.ylabel('Membership')
plt.xlabel("Speed (Miles Per Hour)")
plt.legend(loc='center right', bbox_to_anchor=(1.25, 0.5),
ncol=1, fancybox=True, shadow=True)
```

Figure 2-10 shows the result.

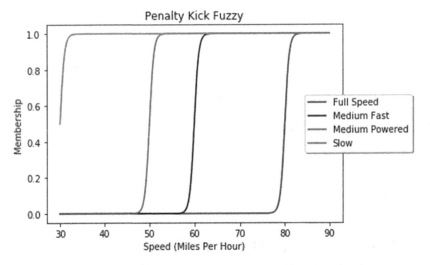

Figure 2-10. *Sigmoidal membership of the soccer example*

It is always a question of debate about which membership function to use. There is no single best answer, but you can use one of the following approaches:

- Look at the distribution of the data, for example, with the help of a histogram. If you cannot deduce patterns from the visualization, it is best to use the triangular or trapezoidal membership functions. Otherwise, use others based on the distribution shape.

- Start the problem with the simple membership functions like triangular or trapezoidal. If they provide good results, all is well and good. Otherwise, move to others, especially Gaussian. Most of the time, the Gaussian membership function will give you the best results.

- Train the model on the membership functions that you want to compare. Later, compare the results using metrics like MAPE (mean average percentage error). Whichever method gives you the lowest error is the best model.

Polynomial Membership Function

The polynomial membership function is basically made up of three types:

- z-shaped

- s-shaped

- pi-shaped

These functions are named based on how each curve looks. They are also called spline-based membership functions. The equations for all three membership functions are explained in the following sections.

Z-Shaped

In this membership function, points a and b represent the extreme portions of the curve. It is an asymmetrical polynomial curve open to the left. Figure 2-11 represents a z-shaped membership function, followed by its equations.

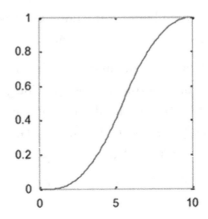

Figure 2-11. *Z-shaped membership function*

$$Z(x;a,b)=\begin{cases} 1, & x\le a \\[2mm] 1-2\left(\dfrac{x-a}{b-a}\right)^2, & a\le x\le \dfrac{a+b}{2} \\[2mm] 2\left(b-\dfrac{x}{b-a}\right)^2, & \dfrac{a+b}{2}\le x\le b \\[2mm] 0, & b\le x \end{cases}$$

Continuing with the soccer example, the following categories will be defined for the Z-shaped membership functions (see Figure 2-12):

- Full speed has a declining point at 80 mph, until 60 mph

- Medium fast has a declining point at 60 mph, until 50 mph

- Medium has a declining point at 50 mph, until 30 mph

- Slow has a declining point at 30 mph, until 20mph

The Python code is as follows:

```
#Importing Necessary Packages
import numpy as np
import skfuzzy as fuzz
import matplotlib.pyplot as plt
%matplotlib inline

#Defining the Fuzzy Range from a speed of 30 to 90
x = np.arange(30, 90, 0.1)

#Defining the z-shaped membership functions
full_speed = fuzz.smf(x, 60,80)
medium_fast = fuzz.smf(x, 50,60)
medium = fuzz.smf(x, 30,50)
slow = fuzz.smf(x, 20,30)

#Plotting the Membership Functions Defined
plt.figure()
plt.plot(x, full_speed, 'b', linewidth=1.5, label='Full Speed')
plt.plot(x, medium_fast, 'k', linewidth=1.5, label='Medium Fast')
plt.plot(x, medium, 'm', linewidth=1.5, label='Medium Powered')
plt.plot(x, slow, 'r', linewidth=1.5, label='Slow')
plt.title('Penalty Kick Fuzzy')
plt.ylabel('Membership')
plt.xlabel("Speed (Miles Per Hour)")
plt.legend(loc='center right', bbox_to_anchor=(1.25, 0.5),
ncol=1, fancybox=True, shadow=True)
```

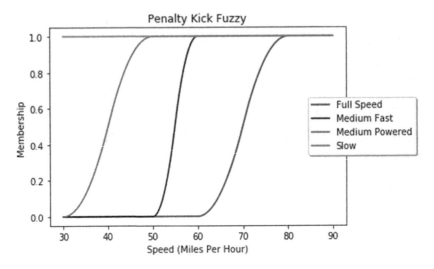

Figure 2-12. *Z-shaped membership of the soccer example*

S-Shaped

In this membership function, points a and b represent the extreme portions of the curve. This is a mirror image of the Z-shaped membership functions, which are open to the right. Figure 2-13 represents an s-shaped membership function, followed by its equations.

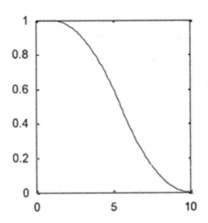

Figure 2-13. *S-shaped membership function*

$$S(x; a, b) = \begin{cases} 0, & x \le a \\ 2\left(\dfrac{x-a}{b-a}\right)^2, & a < x \le \dfrac{a+b}{2} \\ 1 - 2\left(\dfrac{x-b}{b-a}\right)^2, & \dfrac{a+b}{2} < x \le b \\ 1, & x > b \end{cases}$$

The following categories will be defined for the s-shaped membership functions in the soccer example (see Figure 2-14):

- Full speed has an inclining point at 60 mph, until 80 mph

- Medium fast has an inclining point at 50 mph, until 60 mph

- Medium has an inclining point at 30 mph, until 50 mph

- Slow has an inclining point at 20 mph, until 30 mph

The Python code is as follows:

```
#Importing Necessary Packages
import numpy as np
import skfuzzy as fuzz
import matplotlib.pyplot as plt
%matplotlib inline

#Defining the Fuzzy Range from a speed of 30 to 90
x = np.arange(30, 90, 0.1)

#Defining the s-shaped membership functions
full_speed = fuzz.zmf(x, 60,80)
medium_fast = fuzz.zmf(x, 50,60)
medium = fuzz.zmf(x, 30,50)
slow = fuzz.zmf(x, 20,30)
```

```
#Plotting the Membership Functions Defined
plt.figure()
plt.plot(x, full_speed, 'b', linewidth=1.5, label='Full Speed')
plt.plot(x, medium_fast, 'k', linewidth=1.5, label='Medium Fast')
plt.plot(x, medium, 'm', linewidth=1.5, label='Medium Powered')
plt.plot(x, slow, 'r', linewidth=1.5, label='Slow')
plt.title('Penalty Kick Fuzzy')
plt.ylabel('Membership')
plt.xlabel("Speed (Miles Per Hour)")
plt.legend(loc='center right', bbox_to_anchor=(1.25, 0.5),
ncol=1, fancybox=True, shadow=True)
```

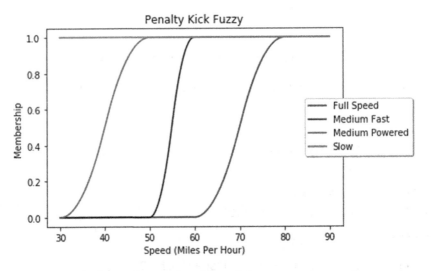

Figure 2-14. *S-shaped membership of the soccer example*

Pi-Shaped

Pi-shaped curves have four parameters. Parameters a and d indicate the feet of the curve, while b and c represent the shoulders. This curve can be defined as a product of the z-shaped and s-shaped membership functions.

It has zero values on both extremes, with a rise in the middle. Figure 2-15 represents a pi-shaped membership function, followed by its equations.

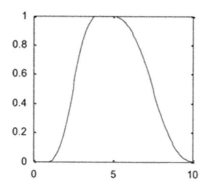

Figure 2-15. *Pi-shaped membership function*

$$\Pi\left(x;a,b,c,d\right)=\begin{cases} 0, & x \le a \\[2mm] 2\left(\dfrac{x-a}{b-a}\right)^{2}, & a \le x \le \dfrac{a+b}{2} \\[2mm] 1-2\left(\dfrac{x-b}{b-a}\right)^{2}, & \dfrac{a+b}{2} \le x \le b \\[2mm] 1 & b \le x \le c \\[2mm] 1-2\left(\dfrac{x-c}{d-c}\right)^{2}, & c \le x \le \dfrac{c+d}{2} \\[2mm] 2\left(\dfrac{x-d}{d-c}\right)^{2}, & \dfrac{c+d}{2} \le x \le d \\[2mm] 0, & x \ge d \end{cases}$$

The following categories will be defined for the z-shaped membership functions (see Figure 2-16):

- Full speed has the feet points defined as [60mph, 100mph] while the shoulder points are defined as [70mph, 80mph]

- Medium fast has the feet points defined as [50mph, 80mph] while shoulder points are defined as [55mph, 60mph]

- Medium has the feet points defined as [30mph, 60mph] while shoulder points are defined as [45mph, 50mph]

- Slow has the feet points defined as [60mph, 100mph] while shoulder points are defined as [70mph, 80mph]

The Python code is as follows:

```
#Importing Necessary Packages
import numpy as np
import skfuzzy as fuzz
import matplotlib.pyplot as plt
%matplotlib inline

#Defining the Fuzzy Range from a speed of 30 to 90
x = np.arange(30, 90, 0.1)

#Defining the pi-shaped membership functions
full_speed = fuzz.pimf(x, 60,70,80,100)
medium_fast = fuzz.pimf(x, 50,55,60,80)
medium = fuzz.pimf(x, 30,45,50,60)
slow = fuzz.pimf(x, 20,25,35,50)

#Plotting the Membership Functions Defined
plt.figure()
plt.plot(x, full_speed, 'b', linewidth=1.5, label='Full Speed')
plt.plot(x, medium_fast, 'k', linewidth=1.5, label='Medium Fast')
plt.plot(x, medium, 'm', linewidth=1.5, label='Medium Powered')
plt.plot(x, slow, 'r', linewidth=1.5, label='Slow')
plt.title('Penalty Kick Fuzzy')
plt.ylabel('Membership')
```

```
plt.xlabel("Speed (Miles Per Hour)")
plt.legend(loc='center right', bbox_to_anchor=(1.25, 0.5),
ncol=1, fancybox=True, shadow=True)
```

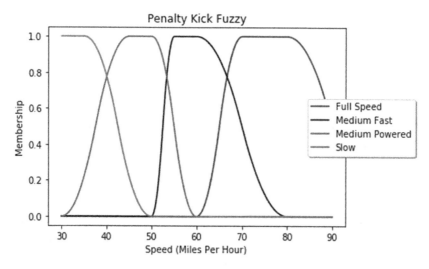

Figure 2-16. *Pi-shaped membership of the soccer example*

Composite and Non-Composite Membership Functions

Projection and cylindrical extension of Fuzzy Sets are the concepts you use when you want to extend a one-dimensional membership function to two-dimensional membership function. These concepts are discussed in the next section on Fuzzy Relations. After applying one of these concepts, you get a 2D membership function. This membership function can be of two types:

- Composite membership function

- Non-composite membership function

A 2D membership function, if it can be broken into two single membership functions, is called a composite membership function. Otherwise, it's called a non-composite membership function.

For example, suppose you have a membership function defined as follows:

$$\mu_A(x,y)=e^{-\left(\frac{x-5}{4}\right)-(y-9)^2}$$

This equation can be broken into two parts:

$$e^{-\left(\frac{x-5}{4}\right)}*e^{(y-9)^2}$$

If you look at this carefully, they are nothing but two Gaussian membership functions. Therefore, you can rewrite them as follows:

$$gaussian(x,5,4)*gaussian(y,9,1)$$

Since you have successfully broken the 2D membership functions to 1D membership functions, this is a composite membership function.

But consider the following equation:

$$\mu_A(x,y)=\frac{1}{1+|x-3||y-4|^7}$$

In this scenario, you won't be able to break it. Hence, it is a non-composite membership function.

Fuzzy Relations

As you learned in the last chapter, there are different kinds of sets—crisp sets and Fuzzy Sets. Whenever you try to determine the relationship between two or more sets, the terminology used is *relation*, and specifically with Fuzzy Sets, this is called *Fuzzy Relation*.

Suppose there are two Fuzzy Sets, X, Y, both belonging to the domain of real numbers and part of a Universe of Discourse.

The Fuzzy Relation, $X \times Y$, will have a relationship defined by this set:

$$R = \{[(x,y), \mu_R(x,y)] \vee (x,y) \in X \times Y\}$$

To represent this relationship in matrix format, consider the following example.

Suppose:

$$X = \{x1, x2, \ldots xn\} \, Y = \{y1, y2, \ldots yn\}$$

The Fuzzy Relation R will be represented by the following matrix:

$$y1y2 \ldots ynx1\mu_R(x1,y1)\mu_R(x1,y2) \ldots \mu_R(x1,yn)x2\mu_R(x2,y1)\mu_R(x2,y2) \ldots$$
$$\mu_R(x2,yn) \ldots xn\mu_R(xn,y1)\mu_R(xn,y2) \ldots \mu_R(xn,yn)$$

Let's look at this concept with an example.

Suppose:

$$X = \{1, 2, 3\} \text{ and } Y = \{1, 2\}$$

If the membership function between the two is given by:

$$\mu R(x,y) = 1/1 + e^{-(x-y)}$$

Using these two formulations, you can define the relationship R as:

$$R = \{ \frac{1/1+}{e^{-(1-1)}} \frac{1/1+}{(1,1),} \frac{1/1+}{e^{-(1-2)}} \frac{1/1+}{(1,2),} \frac{1/1+}{e^{-(2-1)}} \frac{1/1+}{(2,1),} \frac{1/1+}{e^{-(2-2)}} \frac{1/1+}{(2,2),} \frac{1/1+}{e^{-(3-1)}} \frac{1/1+}{(3,1),} e^{-(3-2)}(3,2)\}$$

$$R = \left\{ \begin{array}{l} (0.5 \vee (1,1)), (0.27 \vee (1,2)), (0.73 \vee (2,1)), (0.5 \vee (2,2)), \\ (0.88 \vee (3,1)), (0.5 \vee (3,2)) \end{array} \right\}$$

If you want to represent this relation in matrix format, you get the following matrix:

$$[0.500.270.730.500.880.50]$$

Now you know what a Fuzzy Relation is. The next section looks at some of its properties.

Properties of Fuzzy Relations

This section discusses the following properties of Fuzzy Relations:

- Projection

- Cylindrical extension

- Reflexive relation

- Anti-reflexive relation

- Symmetric relation

- Anti-symmetric relation

- Transitive relation

- Similarity relation

- Anti-similarity relation

- Weak similarity relation

- Order relation

- Pre-order relation

- Half order relation

Projection of Fuzzy Relation

Because a crisp relation is defined in the product space of two or more sets, the concept of *projection* was proposed. Suppose you have a Fuzzy Relation represented by the following matrix:

$$R = [0.10.20.40.20.40.80.40.81]$$

This is the same matrix you got in the previous section, with columns representing members of the X set, and rows representing members of the Y set. Individual values are the membership function's values. Now, if you want to project this relation onto X or Y, it can be defined as follows:

$$R_1 \left(\text{Projection onto X} \right) = \left\{ \left(x, \underset{y}{\max} \, \mu_R(x,y) \right) \middle| (x,y) \in X \times Y \right\}$$

$$R_2 \left(\text{Projection onto Y} \right) = \left\{ \left(y, \underset{x}{\max} \, \mu_R(x,y) \right) \middle| (x,y) \in X \times Y \right\}$$

When you apply both projections to this matrix, you get the following results:

$$\mu_{R1}(x1) = (0.1, 0.2, 0.4) = 0.4$$

$$\mu_{R1}(x2) = (0.2, 0.4, 0.8) = 0.8$$

$$\mu_{R1}(x3) = (0.4, 0.8, 1) = 1$$

Therefore, R_1 becomes:

$$x_2, 0.8\}, (x_3, 1)$$
$$(x_1, 0.4),$$
$$R_1 =$$

Similarly, you can get R2 values as follows:

$$\mu_{R1}(y1) = (0.1, 0.2, 0.4) = 0.4$$

$$\mu_{R1}(y2) = (0.2, 0.4, 0.8) = 0.8$$

$$\mu_{R1}(y3) = (0.4, 0.8, 1) = 1$$

$$y, 0.8\}, (y_3, 1)$$
$$(y_1, 0.4),$$
$$R_2 =$$

Remember, for projection onto X, you do a row-wise comparison. But for projection onto Y, you do a column-wise comparison.

Cylindrical Extension of Fuzzy Relations

Once you have the projection of relation on two sets, you directly refill the values of the original matrix with the membership values. That is called a cylindrical extension of a Fuzzy Relation. It is represented by:

$$cylA(x,y) = A(x)$$

$$\forall x \in X$$

$$\forall y \in Y$$

You can understand this better by extending the previous example.

You got the R_1 and R_2 values. Now you just redefine the matrix with the combined values:

$$R_1 = \begin{bmatrix} 0.40.4 \\ 0.80.8 \\ 11 \end{bmatrix}$$

$$R_2 = \begin{bmatrix} 0.40.4 \\ 0.80.8 \\ 11 \end{bmatrix}$$

Reflexive Relation

If the Fuzzy Relation between two same sets is R, such that for each same value combination, you have a membership function value of 1, then you call the relation *reflexive*. Therefore, if R is a Fuzzy Relation, it will be reflexive if:

$$\mu_R(x,x) = 1 \forall x \in X$$

For example, if X = {1,2,3,4}, the Relation R will be equal to:

$$R = \begin{bmatrix} 10.90.60.2 \\ 0.910.70.3 \\ 0.60.710.9 \\ 0.20.30.91 \end{bmatrix}$$

As you can see, the diagonals of this matrix are 1, proving it to be a reflexive relation.

Anti-Reflexive Relation

If the Fuzzy Relation between two same sets is R, such that for each same value combination, you have a membership function value of 0, then you call the relation *anti-reflexive*. It is represented by:

$$\mu_R(x,x) = 0 \forall x \in X$$

For example, if X = {1,2,3}, then the Relation R will be equal to:

$$R = \begin{bmatrix} 00 & 0.6 \\ 0.3 & 00 \\ 00.3 & 0 \end{bmatrix}$$

As you can see, the diagonals of this matrix are 0, proving it to be an anti-reflexive relation.

Symmetric Relation

If you have two or more members of a Fuzzy Set, x, y, belonging to same set X, and if the membership function value of relation between x and y is the same as the membership function value of relation between y and x, you call the relation a symmetric relation.

$$\mu_R(x,y) = \mu_R(y,x) \forall x, y \in X$$

For example, if X = {1,2,3}, then:

$$\text{If, } R = \begin{bmatrix} 0.8 & 0.1 & 0.7 \\ 0.1 & 1 & 0.6 \\ 0.7 & 0.6 & 0.5 \end{bmatrix}$$

This is a symmetric relation because $\mu_R(x, y)$ and $\mu_R(y, x)$ have the same values.

Anti-Symmetric Relation

If you have two or more members of a Fuzzy Set, x, y, belonging to the same set X, and if the membership function value of relation between x and y is greater than 0, and the membership function value of relation between y and x is 0, you call this an anti-symmetric relation.

If $\mu_R(x, y) > 0$, then $\mu_R(y, x) = 0$, $\forall x, y \in X$, and $x \neq y$.

For example:

$$If\ R = \begin{bmatrix} 000.7 \\ 0.100 \\ 00.60 \end{bmatrix}$$

This is an anti-symmetric relation, because when $\mu_R(x, y) > 0$, then $\mu_R(y, x) = 0$.

Transitive Relation

A Fuzzy Relation is transitive if:

$$\mu_R(x,z) \geq \max\Big(\min\big(\mu_R(x,y),\mu_R(y,z)\big)\Big) x,z \in X$$

This means that you first need to find the R^2 value using the max-min approach, and then check whether it is not always less than or equal to the original membership matrix of R. If it doesn't follow, the equation is transitive.
Suppose you have a relation matrix as follows:

$$R = \begin{bmatrix} 0.70.90.4 \\ 0.10.30.5 \\ 0.20.10 \end{bmatrix}$$

The first step is to find R^2 value. For this, you use the following steps:

$$R.R = \begin{bmatrix} 0.70.90.4 \\ 0.10.30.5 \\ 0.20.10 \end{bmatrix} \cdot \begin{bmatrix} 0.70.90.4 \\ 0.10.30.5 \\ 0.20.10 \end{bmatrix}$$

$$= \begin{bmatrix} max\{min(0.7,0.7)min(0.9,0.1)min(0.4,0.2)\} \\ max\{min(0.7,0.9)min(0.9,0.3)min(0.4,0.1)\} \\ max\{min(0.7,0.4)min(0.9,0.5)min(0.4,0)\} \\ max\{min(0.1,0.7)min(0.3,0.1)min(0.5,0.2)\} \\ max\{min(0.1,0.9)min(0.3,0.3)min(0.5,0.1)\} \\ max\{min(0.1,0.4)min(0.3,0.5)min(0.5,0)\} \\ max\{min(0.2,0.7)min(0.1,0.1)min(0,0.2)\} \\ max\{min(0.2,0.9)min(0.1,0.3)min(0,0.1)\} \\ max\{min(0.2,0.4)min(0.1,0.5)min(0,0)\} \end{bmatrix}$$

Applying the max-min composition, you get the following matrix:

$$R^2 = \begin{bmatrix} 0.70.70.5 \\ 0.10.30.5 \\ 0.20.10 \end{bmatrix}$$

You can see that the values are sometimes greater than the original matrix. Therefore, the matrix is not transitive.

Similarity Relation

If there are two Fuzzy Sets, which are reflexive, symmetric, and transitive, the relation is a *similarity relation*.

$$R = \begin{bmatrix} 10.210.60.20.6 \\ 0.210.20.20.80.2 \\ 10.210.60.20.6 \\ 0.60.20.610.20.8 \\ 0.20.80.20.210.2 \\ 0.60.20.60.80.21 \end{bmatrix}$$

This relation is a similarity relation because:

- $\mu_R(x,x) = 1$

  Which proves that the relation is reflexive.

- $\mu_R(x,y) = \mu_R(y,x)$

  Which proves that the relation is symmetric.

- $\mu_R(x,z) \geq ((\mu_R(x,y), \mu_R(y,z)))x,\, y,\, z \in X$

  Which proves that the relation is transitive.

Since it follows all these principles, it is a similarity relation.

Anti-Similarity Relation

The complement of a similarity relation is an anti-similarity relation. Therefore, you can write it as follows:

$$\mu_{R'} = 1 - \mu_R(x,y)$$

Suppose:

$$\text{If R} = \begin{bmatrix} 10.10.7 \\ 0.110.7 \\ 0.70.71 \end{bmatrix}$$

$$\text{Then } \mu_{R'}(x,y) = 1 - \begin{bmatrix} 10.10.7 \\ 0.110.7 \\ 0.70.71 \end{bmatrix}$$

This is equal to this matrix:

$$\begin{bmatrix} 00.90.3 \\ 0.900.3 \\ 0.30.30 \end{bmatrix}$$

You can say that this is anti-reflexive, symmetric, and transitive. Therefore, R is an anti-similarity relation.

Weak Similarity Relation

If a relation is reflexive and symmetric, but not transitive, the relation is called a weak similarity relation.

$$\text{If R} = \begin{bmatrix} 10.10.80.20.30.1 \\ 100.310.80 \\ 10.700.20.30.7 \\ 10.60.3100.61 \end{bmatrix}$$

When you apply the rules of reflexive, symmetric, and transitive relations, you can see that it is following the first two, but not following the transitive relation property. Therefore, you can say that it is a weak similarity relation.

Half Order Relation

Before talking about a half order relation, you must know what a weak anti-symmetric relation means. This Fuzzy Relation follows these rules:

If

$$\mu_R(x,y) > 0$$

$$\mu_R(y,x) > 0$$

Then

$$x = y$$

Now that you know about it, a half order relation is reflexive as well as weakly symmetric. For example, if

$$R = \begin{bmatrix} 1 & 1.8 & 0.2 & 0.6 & 0.6 & 0.4 \\ 0 & 1 & 0 & 0 & 0.6 & 0 \\ 0 & 0 & 1 & 0 & 0.5 & 0 \\ 0 & 0 & 0 & 1 & 0.6 & 0.4 \\ 0 & 0 & 0 & 0 & 1 & 0 \\ 0 & 0 & 0 & 0 & 0 & 1 \end{bmatrix}$$

Then this relation follows the property of half order relation.

Fuzzy Rules

In Fuzzy Logic, if you want to incorporate conditional statements, you use Fuzzy Rules (see Figure 2-17). The most important thing to understand is the Fuzzy If-Then Rules. A single sample Fuzzy Rule looks like this:

If x is A then y is B

In this statement, A and B are called linguistic values. These are the values that assume that it has been derived from statistical research, a mathematical model, etc. For example, it can take categorical values (good, average, or best), probabilistic values (0.1, 0.3, or 0.9), or any other part of an experiment. These values can be part of a Fuzzy Set, which can be a member of the Universe of Discourse X and Y.

If you break the previous statement into two halves:

- x is A

- y is B

The first part is called an *antecedent* or *premise*, while the second part is called the *consequent* or *conclusion* (see Figure 2-2).

For example, consider the following rules:

- If road is good then condition of car is good

- If company is good then employees are satisfied

- If service is good then tip is average

As stated, *A* and *B* are Fuzzy Sets, so they have a value between 0 and 1. That means you provide a value between 0 and 1 as the antecedent, and you get a value from 0 to 1 as the consequent. So, in the previous example, good can be assigned a number between 0 and 1, and you'll get a response between 0 and 1, which will represent good, average, or satisfied, based on the problem statement.

When you apply If-Then Rules, then input is set as a value between 0 and 1, but the output is an entire Fuzzy Set. After this, you need to apply one of the Fuzzy Operations, called Defuzzification, which then gives you a crisp output value between 0 and 1.

The process of the If-Then Rule involves:

1. Reading the antecedent

2. Converting the input to a Fuzzy Set

3. Applying the necessary Fuzzy Operators

4. Applying the result to a consequent

5. Getting a Fuzzy Set as output

6. Defuzzifying to get a crisp answer

These examples are binary. Antecedents and consequents can both have multiple parts. For example:

- **If** sky is gray **and** wind is strong **and** barometer is falling, **then** ...

- If temperature is cold then hot water valve is open and cold water valve is shut

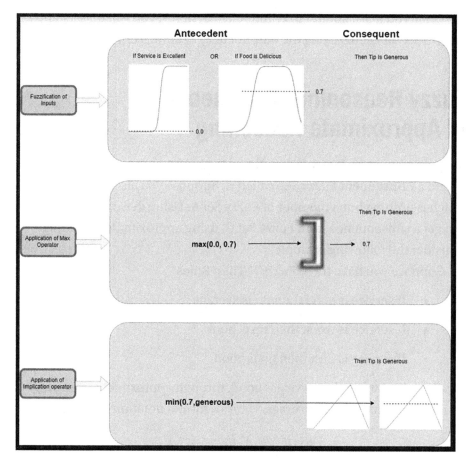

Figure 2-17. *Fuzzy Rules in a service example*

With this logic, the rules can be divided into two parts:

- *Fuzzy Mapping Rule.* This rule first Fuzzified the antecedent inputs, in this case, service and food, and then applied the max operator. This gives the final crisp value that needs to be sent to the consequent.

- *Fuzzy Implication Rule.* In this rule, the consequent receives the crisp input from the antecedent, and then it decides what the Fuzzy Set will look like. You get a Fuzzy Set as output after this step.

79

Once you learn about Fuzzy Inference Systems, you will understand the process of Defuzzifying the output Fuzzy Set into a crisp set.

Fuzzy Reasoning: The Theory of Approximate Reasoning

Say you know some Fuzzy Rules related to an Antecedent Fuzzy Set, called A, and a Consequent Fuzzy Set, called C. Suppose you also know a fact, which is nothing but a member of Fuzzy Set A. Using these rules, you can get a consequence from Fuzzy Set C, using approximate reasoning. Consider the following example.

Suppose you have three Fuzzy If-Then Rules:

- If service is good then tip is average

- If service is worst then tip is poor

- If service is best then tip is good

If you know that the service is good, through approximate reasoning, you can say that the tip is average. Here's a formal notation of this idea.

$$R1 : if \ x \ is \ A1 \ then \ y \ is \ C1,$$

$$R2 : if \ x \ is \ A2 \ then \ y \ is \ C2,$$

$$\ldots\ldots\ldots$$

$$Rn : if \ x \ is \ A_n \ then \ y \ is \ C_n$$

$$: ! x \ is \ A$$

$$so, consequence : y \ is \ C$$

Now that you know the basics, let's look at some formal definitions related to Fuzzy Reasoning:

- Entailment rule

- Conjunction rule

- Disjunction rule

- Projection rule

- Negation rule

- Generalized modus ponens

- Generalized modus tollens

Entailment Rule

If you know that service is poor, and poor is a subset of bad, you can say that the service is bad. This is called an entailment rule, represented by:

$$x \text{ is } A$$

$$A \subset B$$

$$x \text{ is } B$$

Conjunction Rule

This can also be called the AND rule. If service is not very good and service is not very bad, you can say that service is not very good and not very bad. This is called a conjunction rule, and it's represented by:

$$x \text{ is } A$$
$$\frac{x \text{ is } B}{x \text{ is } A \cap B}$$

Disjunction Rule

This can also be called the OR rule. If service is not very good or service is not very bad, you can say that service is not very good or not very bad. This is called a conjunction rule, and it's represented by:

$$\begin{array}{c} x \ is \ A \\ \underline{x \ is \ B} \\ x \ is \ A \cup B \end{array}$$

Projection Rule

If you have two members of Fuzzy Set $X \wedge Y$: x, y respectively, and you have a relation R between them, then you can define a projection rule on them.

If you say that (x, y) is close to $(4, 5)$, then you can conclude that x is close to 4 and y is close to 5.

Negation Rule

If you say that x is *high*, but a fact disproves it by saying, *not(x is high)*, then you can conclude using the negation rule that x is *not high*. This can be represented by:

$$\frac{not\left(x \ is \ A\right)}{x \ is \neg A}$$

Generalized Modus Ponens

You know that if the service is poor, the tip is bad. You also know as a fact that the service is good. Keeping those two situations in mind, you can say that the tip is nice, considering nice is a complement of bad, and good is a complement of poor. This is what the generalized modus ponens (GMP) says. Here it is in representation format:

$$if \ x \ is \ A \ then \ y \ is \ B \rightarrow Premise$$

$$x \ is \ A' \rightarrow !$$

$$y \ is \ B' \rightarrow Consequence$$

There are some properties that GMP needs to follow.
Basic property:

$$x \ is \ A \ then \ y \ is \ B \rightarrow Premise$$

$$x \ is \ A \rightarrow !$$

$$y \ is \ B \rightarrow Consequence$$

Total Indeterminacy property:

$$x \ is \ A \ then \ y \ is \ B \rightarrow Premise$$

$$x \ is \ \neg A \rightarrow !$$

$$y \ is \ Unknown \rightarrow Consequence$$

Subset property:

$$x \ is \ A \ then \ y \ is \ B \rightarrow Premise$$

$$x \ is \ A' \subset A \rightarrow !$$

$$y \ is \ B \rightarrow Consequence$$

Superset property:

$$x \text{ is } A \text{ then } y \text{ is } B \rightarrow Premise$$

$$x \text{ is } A' \rightarrow !$$

$$y \text{ is } B' \supset B \rightarrow Consequence$$

Generalized Modus Tollens

Again, if you know that the service is good, that means the tip is nice. You also know as a fact that the tip is bad. Keeping these two situations in mind, you can say that the service is poor, considering bad is a complement of nice, and poor is a complement of good. This is what the generalized modus tollens says:

$$if \ x \text{ is } A \text{ then } y \text{ is } B \rightarrow Premise$$

$$y \text{ is } B' \rightarrow !$$

$$x \text{ is } A' \rightarrow Consequence$$

Aggregation in Fuzzy System Modeling

Before look at aggregation, you must know the steps required for any Fuzzy Inference Process:

1. Whatever the input is, you must match every rule with it.

2. Determine the output of every rule as a Fuzzy Set.

3. Aggregate all the rule outputs to get the overall Fuzzy System output Fuzzy Set.

4. Perform an action based on the output Fuzzy Set.

The consideration in this section is the third point: aggregation of the output rules. You can represent this operation as follows:

$$F(y) = Agg\left(R_1(y), R_2(y), \ldots R_n(y)\right)$$

In the previous equation, *Agg* represented the aggregation operator. All the parameters present inside the operator are the membership grades of the output rules for every value of y present in Fuzzy Set Y.

For aggregation operations, the following three conditions need to be satisfied:

- Commutativity
- Monotonicity
- Fixed identity

Commutativity

All the elements on which the aggregation operation is going to be performed can be unordered and can contain duplicate values. This means that indexing doesn't play a role here. So R1 can come after R45, which can come after R2.

Monotonicity

Suppose there are two elements, y1 and y2. You know that R(y1) and R(y2) represent the degree of membership. This tells you the probability of y1 being the correct solution versus y2 being correct. If all the rules applied on y1 and y2 state that R(y1) ≥ R(y2), the overall system will prefer y1 over y2. This can be represented by the monotonicity condition:

$$R_j(y1) \geq R_j(y2)$$

This means that, for all the values of j, the membership of y1 will be greater than or equal to the membership of y2.

Fixed Identity

Suppose there are few rules that don't ensure an output. In that scenario, these rules will not affect the output of all the other rules, which do determine potential outputs. This is the property of fixed identity.

When you combine all three conditions, the aggregation is called Monotonic Identity Commutative Aggregation (MICA). The following is a list of the MICA operators:

- Triangular norms

- Triangular Co-Norms

- Averaging and Compensatory operators

Triangular Norms

The intersection of two Fuzzy Sets can be represented by triangular norms (aka T-Norms, shown in Figure 2-18). If you have two Fuzzy Sets A and B, their intersection can be defined by:

$$\mu_{A \cap B}(x) = T\left(\mu_A(x), \mu_B(x)\right)$$

This intersection operator has the following characteristics:

- Boundary

- Monotonicity

- Commutativity

- Associativity

Boundary:

$$T(0,0) = 0$$

$$T(a,1) = T(1,a) = a$$

Monotonicity:

$$T(a,b) \leq T(c,d) \; if \; a \leq c \wedge b \leq d$$

Commutativity:

$$T(a,b) = T(b,a)$$

Associativity:

$$x, T(y,z) = T(T(x,y),z)$$
$$T$$

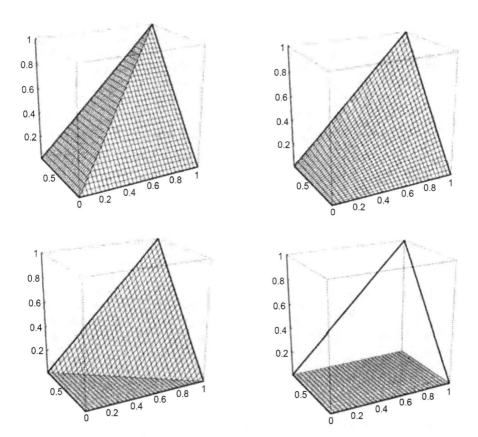

Figure 2-18. *Minimum, Product, Lukasiewicz, and Drastic Product T-Norms*

There are different types of triangular norms used in various applications. Some of them are:

Minimum T-Norm:

$$T_M(x,y) = \min(x,y)$$

Product T-Norm:

$$T_P(x,y) = x.y$$

Lukasiewicz T-Norm:

$$T_L(x,y) = \max(x+y-1,0)$$

Drastic Product T-Norm (the weakest t-norm):

$$T_D(x,y) = \{if(x,y) \in (0,1)^2 \ otherwise$$

Out of all these triangular norms, the Drastic Product T-Norm is considered the smallest one, while the Minimum T-Norm is considered the largest one. The Minimum T-Norm treats each member as an idempotent element. The Product T-Norm is considered a strict T-Norm, while the Lukasiewicz is considered a nilpotent t-norm. The following code shows the Python implementation of these triangular norms. It finds the triangular norm of the two Fuzzy Sets defined earlier—full speed and slow.

```
import numpy as np
#Defining the T-Norm Function
def t_norm(mfx,mfy):
    tnorm = np.fmin(mfx, mfy)
    return tnorm
#Defining sigmoidal membership function
full_speed = fuzz.sigmf(x, 80,2)
slow = fuzz.sigmf(x, 30,2)
```

```
#Finding the Intersection
t_norm(full_speed,slow)
```

You have looked at the different properties of T-Norms, as well as their types. Later chapters include their applications. For now, one thing should be clear that T-Norms are used when you find the intersection between two Fuzzy Sets.

Triangular Co-Norms

The union of two Fuzzy Sets can be represented by triangular Co-Norms (aka T-Co-Norm, shown in Figure 2-19). If you have two Fuzzy Sets A and B, their intersection can be defined by:

$$\mu_{A \cup B}(x) = S\big(\mu_A(x), \mu_B(x)\big)$$

This intersection operator has the following characteristics:

- Boundary
- Monotonicity
- Commutativity
- Associativity

Boundary:

$$S(0,0) = 0$$

$$S(a,0) = S(0,a) = a$$

Monotonicity:

$$S(a,b) \leq S(c,d) \, if \, a \leq c \wedge b \leq d$$

Commutativity:

$$S(a,b) = S(b,a)$$

Associativity:

$$x, S(y,z) = S(S(x,y),z)$$
$$S$$

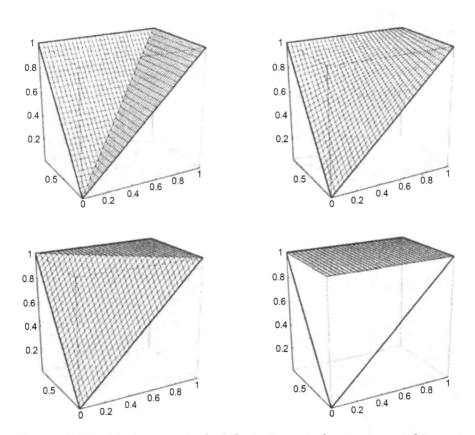

Figure 2-19. *Maximum, Probabilistic Sum, Lukasiewicz, and Drastic Sum Bounded T-Co-Norms*

There are different types of triangular co-norms used in various applications. Some of them are:

Maximum T-Co-Norm:

$$S_M(x,y) = max(x,y)$$

Probabilistic Sum T-Co-Norm:

$$S_P(x,y) = x + y - x.y$$

Lukasiewicz T-Co-Norm:

$$S_L(x,y) = min(x+y,1)$$

Drastic Sum Bounded Sum T-Co-Norm (Strongest T-Co-Norm):

$$S_D(x,y) = \{if(x,y) \in (0,1)^2$$

$$max(x,y) otherwise$$

The following code shows the Python implementation of these Triangular Co-Norms. It finds the triangular Co-Norm of the two Fuzzy Sets defined before—full speed and slow.

```python
import numpy as np
#Defining the T-Conorm Function
def t_conorm(mfx,mfy):
    tnorm = np.fmax(mfx, mfy)
    return tnorm
#Defining sigmoidal membership function
full_speed = fuzz.sigmf(x, 80,2)
slow = fuzz.sigmf(x, 30,2)
#Finding the Intersection
t_conorm(full_speed,slow)
```

Summary

This chapter explained membership functions in detail. It covered the different types of membership functions and explained how they are used. Because it's sometimes tricky to determine which membership function to use, this chapter discussed a few approaches. The chapter also applied every membership function in Python. It then moved on to Fuzzy Rules and explained how they are applied. The chapter concluded by explaining the Fuzzy T-Norm and T-Co-Norm operators.

The next chapter discusses the Fuzzy Inference System in detail. The chapter discusses how all these processes are used and how they form a complete structure.

CHAPTER 3

Fuzzy Inference Systems

The previous two chapters explained the core concepts related to Fuzzy Logic. They discussed Fuzzy Sets and how they are different from the classical/crisp sets. You also learned about various operations that can be done on them and their properties. Then you learned about membership functions, which define the membership values of each element present in a Fuzzy Set. You learned about the different types of membership functions. Later, you learned about the Fuzzy Rules and reasoning approaches that utilize the concepts of membership functions to give various Fuzzy Solutions.

This chapter looks at real applications of all the concepts that you have learned so far. The chapter covers different types of Fuzzy Inference Systems, through which various real-life problems are solved in the industry. To understand these systems, you first need to understand the processes of Fuzzification and Defuzzification. You have already seen the Fuzzification process in the previous chapter, when you found the membership function values of each element of a set to make it a member of a Fuzzy Set. This chapter starts with the concept of Defuzzification and then moves on to different Fuzzy Inference Systems.

© Himanshu Singh, Yunis Ahmad Lone 2020
H. Singh and Y. A. Lone, *Deep Neuro-Fuzzy Systems with Python*,
https://doi.org/10.1007/978-1-4842-5361-8_3

Defuzzification

Defuzzification is the process of converting a Fuzzy Set into a crisp set. You know that in most applications you have to use Fuzzy Sets, as people's opinions are never crisp. But when you incorporate these Fuzzy values and have to make a decision, you must convert the Fuzzy output into crisp values. Therefore, Defuzzification helps convert output given in a Fuzzy Set to crisp values. If control system functioning depends on input, the process of Defuzzification determines what exactly needs to be done once that input is provided. The general process of a Fuzzy System, of which Defuzzification is a part, is illustrated in Figure 3-1.

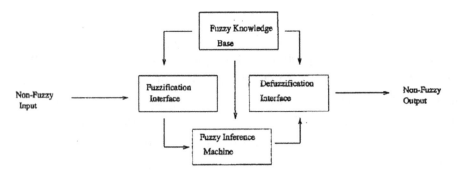

Figure 3-1. *The process of a Fuzzy Inference System*

Formally, you can define the Defuzzification process as follows:

"A Defuzzification method on a certain referential set V as a mapping from the class of fuzzy Subsets of V into V. A nonrestrictive coherence condition is that the associated point must belong to the support of the original fuzzy subset."

There are different types of Defuzzification approaches. The most common ones are shown in Figure 3-2.

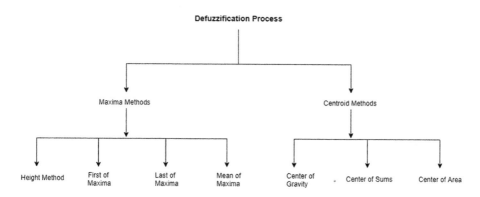

Figure 3-2. *Types of Defuzzifiers*

The following sections discuss the different types of Defuzzification methods.

λ CUT METHOD

Suppose you have a Fuzzy Set given by:

$$A = \left\{ \frac{1}{a}, \frac{0.9}{b}, \frac{0.6}{c}, \frac{0.3}{d}, \frac{0.01}{e}, \frac{0}{f}, \right\}$$

It can be represented as a discrete graph, as shown in Figures 3-3 through 3-9.

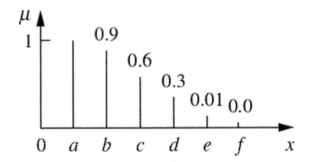

Figure 3-3. *Discrete representation of Fuzzy Set A*

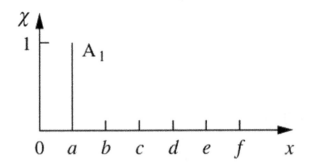

Figure 3-4. *Discrete representation of Fuzzy Set A_1*

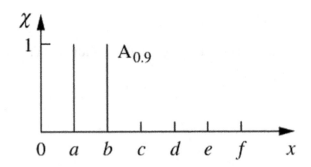

Figure 3-5. *Discrete representation of Fuzzy Set $A_{0.9}$*

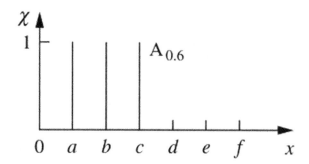

Figure 3-6. *Discrete representation of Fuzzy Set $A_{0.6}$*

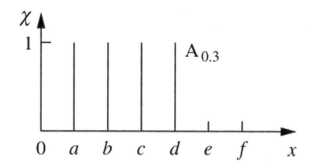

Figure 3-7. *Discrete representation of Fuzzy Set $A_{0.3}$*

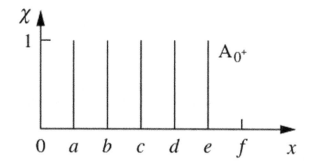

Figure 3-8. *Discrete representation of Fuzzy Set A_{0^+}*

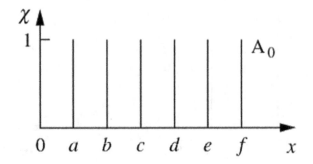

Figure 3-9. *Discrete representation of Fuzzy Set A_0*

You can produce different crisp sets derived from different values of lambda $(1, 0.9, 0.6, 0.3, 0^+, 0)$:

$$A_1 = \{a\}$$

$$A_{0.9} = \{a,b\}$$

$$A_{0.6} = \{a,b,c\}$$

$$A_{0.3} = \{a,b,c,d\}$$

$$A_{0^+} = \{a,b,c,d,e\}$$

$$A_0 = \{A\}$$

If you define λ-cut sets using Fuzzy Set notation, you'll get something like this:

$$A_{0.9} = \left\{ \frac{1}{a}, \frac{1}{b}, \frac{0}{c}, \frac{0}{d}, \frac{0}{e}, \frac{0}{f} \right\}$$

Consider the properties of λ-cuts:

1. $\left(A \cup B\right)_\lambda = A_\lambda \cup B_\lambda$

2. $\left(A \cap B\right)_\lambda = A_\lambda \cap B_\lambda$

3. $\left(\underline{A}\right)_\lambda \neq \underline{A}_\lambda$ except for the λ value of 0.5

4. $A_\alpha \subseteq A_\lambda$ where, $\lambda \leq \alpha \mid 0 \leq \alpha \leq 1 \mid A_0 = X$

If you visualize this using a Sigmoid membership function, you get the diagrams in Figures 3-10 and 3-11.

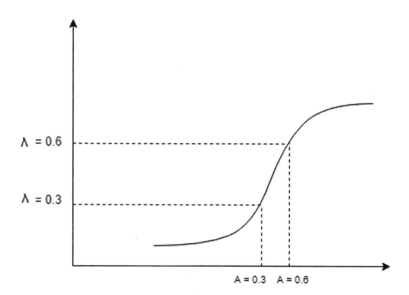

Figure 3-10. *Sigmoid membership function*

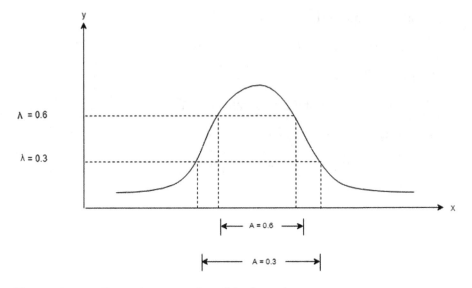

Figure 3-11. *Gaussian membership function*

Consider another example:

$$A = \left\{ \frac{0.9}{x_1}, \frac{0.5}{x_2}, \frac{0.2}{x_3}, \frac{0.3}{x_4} \right\}$$

Based on the previous computation, you would get $A_{0.6}$ as:

$$\therefore A_{0.6} = \left\{ \frac{1}{x_1}, \frac{0}{x_2}, \frac{0}{x_3}, \frac{0}{x_4} \right\} = x_1$$

Max Membership Principle/Height Method

This method is used only when the output membership function has peaks (for example, the triangular membership functions).

$$\mu_A\left(Z^*\right) \geq \mu_A\left(Z\right) \text{ for all } z \in Z$$

Formally, it obtains Z_0 as a weighted average of all the representative points z_i of C_i by the heights h_i of C'_i. This can be represented mathematically as:

$$Z^* = \frac{h_1\,z_1 + h_2\,z_2 + \ldots + h_i\,z_i}{h_1 + h_2 + \ldots + h_i}$$

Z^* is the Defuzzified value, also known as the output of Fuzzy Set A. One important point is that height should be considered unique in this method (see Figure 3-12).

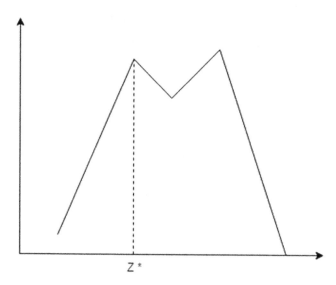

Figure 3-12. *Height method*

First/Last/Mean of Maximum Method

This method takes the union of all the possible Fuzzy Outputs and finds the smallest value with the maximum membership degree.

$$First\ of\ Maximum = z^* = z \in Zinf\left\{z \in Z \mid \mu_c(z) = hgt(c)\right\}$$

$$Last\ of\ Maximum = z^* = z \in Zsup\left\{z \in Z \mid \mu_c(z) = hgt(c)\right\}$$

$$hgt(c) = z \in Zsup\left\{\mu_c(z)\right\}$$

In the previous equation, *hgt(c)* represents the highest height present in the diagram of the union. You can better understand this with an example. Suppose the output membership function looks like the graph in Figure 3-13.

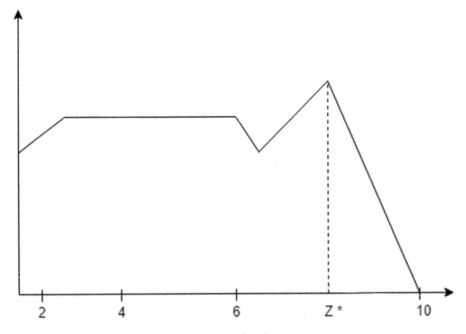

Figure 3-13. *Last of maximum method*

Now, based on these equations, you can see that the highest peak comes at 8. Either it is the first of the maximum method or the last of the maximum method.

Center of Gravity Method or Centroid Method

This method considers the entire Fuzzy Output and finds the centroid of it to give you the Defuzzified output. This can be represented by the following formula:

$$z^* = \frac{\int \mu_A(z).z.dz}{\int \mu_A(z).dz}$$

For a discrete set of values, the formula is revised as follows:

$$z^* = \frac{\sum_{i=1}^{n} A_i * x_i}{\sum_{i=1}^{n} A_i}$$

where A represents the sub-areas and x represents the centroid.

You can better understand this concept with the help of Figure 3-14.

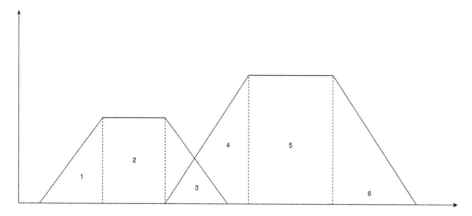

Figure 3-14. *COG method*

You can see in the diagram in Figure 3-14 that the membership functions can be divided into six separate areas. When you're using the Center of Gravity method, you need to determine the centroid and the areas of each specific sub-area. Start by determining the areas:

- The total area of sub-area 6 is ½ * 2 * 0.5 = 0.5

- The total area of sub-area 5 is (7-3) * 0.5 = 4 * 0.5 = 2

- The total area of the sub-area 4 is ½ * (7.5-7) * 0.2 = 0.5 * 0.5 * 0.2 =.05

- The total area of sub-area 3 is 0.5 * 0.3 = .15

- The total area of sub-area 2 is 0.5 * 0.3 = .15

- The total area of sub-area 1 is ½ * 1 * 0.3 = .15

The second step is to determine the centroid:

- The centroid of sub-area 6 is (1+3+3)/3 = 7/3 = 2.333

- The centroid of sub-area 5 is (7+3)/2 = 10/2 = 5

- The centroid of sub-area 4 is (7+7+7.5)/3 = 21.5/3 = 7.166

- The centroid of sub-area 3 is (7+7.5)/2 = 14.5/2 = 7.25

- The centroid of sub-are 2 is (7.5+8)/2 = 15.5/2 = 7.75

- The centroid of sub-area 1 is (8+8+9)/3 = 25/3 = 8.333

Now, using the formula that you already learned about, you can get the Defuzzified value as follows:

$$\frac{1.665+10+0.3583+1.0875+1.1625+1.2499}{0.5+2+0.05+0.15+0.15+0.15} = 5.008$$

Therefore, z^*=5.008.

Weighted Average Method

This method is considered faster in computation and is mainly used in the Sugeno and Tsukamoto Fuzzy Inference Systems. It is represented by the following formula:

$$Z^* = \frac{\sum \mu_A(\overline{Z}).\overline{Z}}{\sum \mu_A(\overline{Z})}$$

Figure 3-15 shows this Defuzzification method.

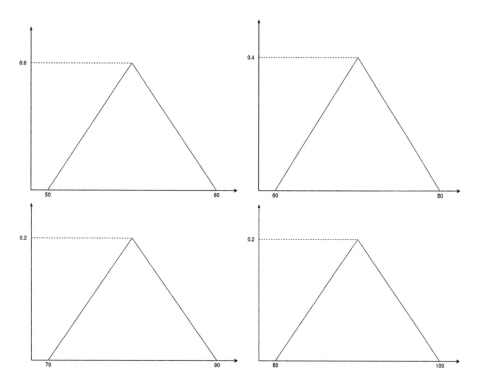

Figure 3-15. *Weighted average method*

The diagram in Figure 3-15 shows four triangular Fuzzy Sets with different membership values. You need to Defuzzify them to a crisp value using the weighted average method. For this, you use the discrete weighted average Defuzzification formula:

$$z^* = \frac{\sum_{i=1}^{n} \mu(x) * x_i}{\sum_{i=1}^{n} \mu(x)}$$

where x represents the element having the maximum membership function. You will get the following results when you apply the formula,

$$\frac{60 * 0.6 + 70 * 0.4 + 80 * 0.2 + 90 * 0.2}{0.6 + 0.4 + 0.2 + 0.2} = 70$$

Center of Sum Method

The Center of Sum Method has the following properties:

- It is one of the fastest Defuzzification approaches.

- It is not limited to symmetric membership functions, unlike other methods. It can be applied to non-symmetric membership functions as well.

This method can be represented by the following formula:

$$z^* = \frac{\int \underline{z} \sum_{k=1}^{n} \mu_A(Z) dz}{\int \sum_{k=1}^{n} \mu_A(Z) dz}$$

$\underline{Z}$ is the distance of the centroid from each membership function.

The Defuzzified value, when you take discrete elements into consideration, is given by this formula:

$$z^* = \frac{\sum_{i=1}^{n} x_i \sum_{k=1}^{n} \mu_{A_k}(x_i)}{\sum_{i=1}^{n} \sum_{k=1}^{n} \mu_{A_k}(x_i)}$$

For example, you can use the same example used for the Center of Gravity approach (see Figure 3-16).

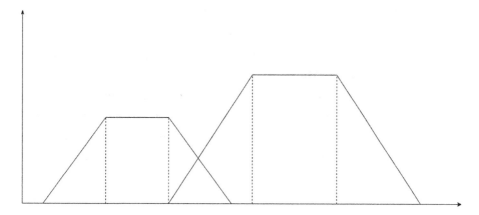

Figure 3-16. *Center of Sum method*

You have two Fuzzy membership functions, therefore you have to consider two areas.

$$A_1 = \frac{1}{2} * \left[(9-3)+(8-4) \right] * 0.3 = \frac{3}{2} = 1.5$$

$$A_2 = \frac{1}{2} * \left[(8-1)+(7-3) \right] * 0.5 = \frac{55}{20} = 2.75$$

Therefore, the Defuzzified value will be:

$$\frac{2.75*5+1.5*6}{2.75+1.5} = 5.35$$

This section doesn't cover all the available Defuzzifiers. The next section starts with the Fuzzy Inference Systems. You will see the Python applications of different Fuzzifiers in that section.

Fuzzy Inference Systems

When you have to design a system that is quite uncertain, one of the best approaches is using Fuzzy Inference Systems. Fuzzy Logic is used when you have a fixed set of rules and need to create systems based on that. But, when you add uncertainties inside the process, it requires some kind of inference of the process from the existing data. Using a Fuzzy Inference System is the way to infer those processes.

A Fuzzy Inference System (FIS) provides a way of mapping an input space to an output space with Fuzzy Logic. FIS tries to mimic the process with which humans solve any problem statement using reasoning. FIS does that by using Fuzzy Logic, especially Fuzzy If-Then rules. Figure 3-17 represents the Fuzzy Inference System structure.

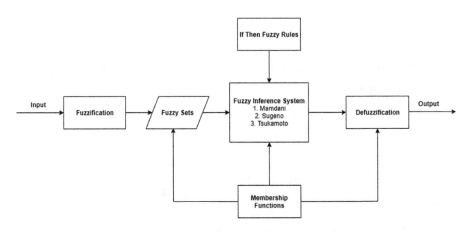

Figure 3-17. *Fuzzy Inference System process*

All the blocks in the diagram in Figure 3-17 are explained here:

- A database of all the Fuzzy If-Then Rules describing a system

- Database of membership functions

- Inference operations on Fuzzy Rules

- Defuzzification of Fuzzy Results into crisp outputs

When you combine all the rules and the membership functions database, it is called a *knowledge base.*

Now that you know the basic structure of the Fuzzy Inference System, you can look at some of its types. Fuzzy Inference Systems can be divided into three types:

- Mamdani model

- Takagi-Sugeno model

- Tsukamoto model

Mamdani Fuzzy Inference System

The Mamdani method is the most widely used Fuzzy Inference System. Because of its simple structure, it is used to solve all general decision-making problems. Mamdani FIS follows these general steps:

1. Step 1: Fuzzify the input.

2. Step 2: Find and evaluate the antecedent of each rule.

3. Step 3: Find the consequent of each rule.

4. Step 4: Aggregate the consequents.

5. Step 5: Defuzzify the results.

First, you convert the crisp inputs to Fuzzy Sets (aka, *Fuzzification*). For each input, you try to find the membership value. Suppose the antecedent has multiple parts. In that case, you use an aggregation operation like T-Norm or T-Co-Norm to get a single membership value.

You can better understand this with the help of an example. Suppose the rulebase says the following:

> "If the product reviews are excellent or the product
> is beautiful."

You can divide the product reviews and the product aesthetics in a rating between 1 and 5. A review of 1 means poor and a review of 5 means excellent. For the product, 1 means a bad design and 5 means an awesome design. Now that you have defined the preliminaries, you can look at the first part: Fuzzification.

If you use sigmoid membership function, the graph will look like Figure 3-18.

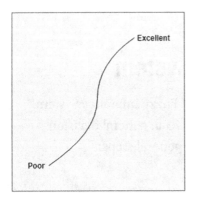 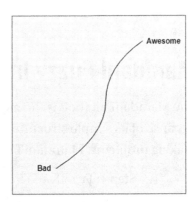

Figure 3-18. *Sigmoid representation*

Suppose you got input about the review as 1, and input about the design as 4. If you apply membership functions over the items, you may get 0.0 in the sigmoid curve for reviews and 0.7 in the sigmoid curve for the product, as shown in Figure 3-19.

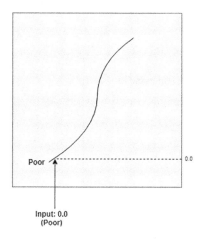
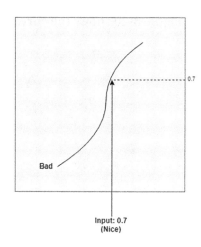

Figure 3-19. *Fuzzification*

Since there is an OR condition in between, that means you must apply the T-co-Norm operator here, which also means you apply the MAX operator.

$$max(0.0, 0.7) = 0.7$$

This is the final membership value for the input part. Suppose the consequents membership function is again sigmoid, and the rule says that:

> "If the antecedent is true, the product is
> recommended."

111

Figure 3-20 shows the curve.

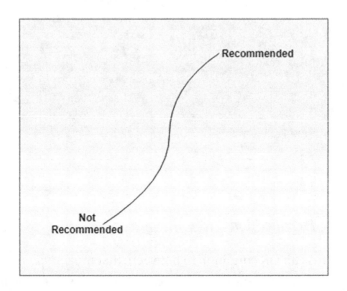

Figure 3-20. *Output membership function*

You can apply one of the implication operators to truncate the consequent membership function. This example uses the MIN operator. Once you get the output, the next step is to aggregate it into a single Fuzzy Set. This can be done using Fuzzy Aggregation Operators (see Figure 3-21).

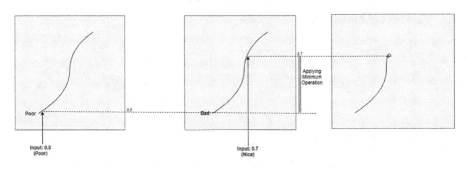

Figure 3-21. *Aggregation*

You might better understand this with the help of some examples, only this time you will take the triangular membership functions as output. Suppose, in the rulebase, you have three Fuzzy If-Then rules:

- If product reviews are excellent or the product is beautiful, the product is recommended.

- If product reviews are good or the product is nice, the product is somewhat recommended.

- If the product reviews are poor or the product is bad looking, the product is not recommended.

Suppose you get the same input as in the previous example: Review = 1 and Design = 4.

Figure 3-22 illustrates the entire process.

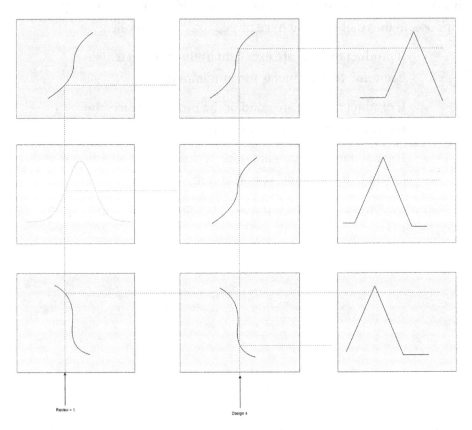

Figure 3-22. *Rulebase*

Now that you have an aggregated Fuzzy Set, the next thing you want is crisp output (see Figure 3-23). This can be done using the Defuzzification approach. There are a lot of Defuzzification approaches, as you have already seen, but the one used here is the Centroid method. So, you need to find the centroid of the aggregation, which is the Center of Area. Using this approach, you find the region with the highest area and then return the Center of Gravity of that area.

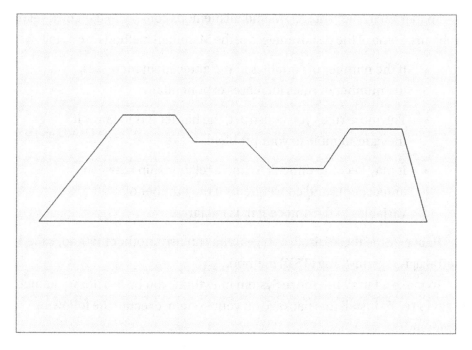

Figure 3-23. *Output aggregated fuzzy*

You can see that c_1 has the largest area. Hence, you will find x' (the center of gravity) fit.

$$x^* = \frac{\int \mu_{c_m}(x).x'dx}{\int \mu_{c_m}(x)dx}$$

With this formula, you get the answer as 13.7%.

The main advantages of using the Mamdani method are as follows:

- It's intuitive

- It enjoys widespread acceptance

- It's well suited for human input

Apart from the advantages, Mamdani methods come with their own set of problems. Some of the disadvantages of the Mamdani methods are as follows:

- If the number of variables in the antecedent increases, the number of rules increases exponentially.

- The more rules you construct, the harder it is to know if they are suitable to your problem.

- It may become difficult to find a relationship between antecedents and consequents if the number of variables in the antecedent is too large.

To overcome these disadvantages, you can use another method, called the Takagi-Sugeno-Kang (TSK) method.

To make a Fuzzy Inference System in Python, you have a library named FuzzyLite. To install this package on your system, execute the following command:

```
pip install pyfuzzylite
```

Fuzzylite is a free and open source Fuzzy Logic control library programmed in C++ for multiple platforms (e.g., Windows, Linux, Mac, and iOS). The goal of the FuzzyLite libraries is to easily design and efficiently operate Fuzzy Logic controllers following an object-oriented programming model, without relying on external libraries. For detailed exploration of this library, clone the GitHub page:

```
https://github.com/fuzzylite/pyfuzzylite.git
```

You can see the application of the Mamdani FIS in Python using this package:

```
import fuzzylite as fl
#Declaring and Initializing the Fuzzy Engine
engine = fl.Engine(
    name="SimpleDimmer",
```

116

```python
    description="Simple Dimmer Fuzzy System which dims light
    based upon Light Conditions"
)
#Defining the Input Variables (Fuzzification)
engine.input_variables = [
    fl.InputVariable(
    name="Ambient",
    description="",
    enabled=True,
    minimum=0.000,
    maximum=1.000,
    lock_range=False,
    terms=[
    fl.Triangle("DARK", 0.000, 0.250, 0.500), #Triangular
    Membership Function defining "Dark"
    fl.Triangle("MEDIUM", 0.250, 0.500, 0.750), #Triangular
    Membership Function defining "Medium"
    fl.Triangle("BRIGHT", 0.500, 0.750, 1.000) #Triangular
    Membership Function defining "Bright"
    ]
    )
]
#Defining the Output Variables (Defuzzification)
engine.output_variables = [
    fl.OutputVariable(
    name="Power",
    description="",
    enabled=True,
    minimum=0.000,
    maximum=1.000,
    lock_range=False,
    aggregation=fl.Maximum(),
```

```
      defuzzifier=fl.Centroid(200),
      lock_previous=False,
      terms=[
      fl.Triangle("LOW", 0.000, 0.250, 0.500), #Triangular
      Membership Function defining "LOW Light"
      fl.Triangle("MEDIUM", 0.250, 0.500, 0.750), #Triangular
      Membership Function defining "MEDIUM light"
      fl.Triangle("HIGH", 0.500, 0.750, 1.000) #Triangular
      Membership Function defining "HIGH Light"
      ]
      )
]
#Creation of Fuzzy Rule Base
engine.rule_blocks = [
      fl.RuleBlock(
      name="",
      description="",
      enabled=True,
      conjunction=None,
      disjunction=None,
      implication=fl.Minimum(),
      activation=fl.General(),
      rules=[
      fl.Rule.create("if Ambient is DARK then Power is HIGH",
      engine),
      fl.Rule.create("if Ambient is MEDIUM then Power is
      MEDIUM", engine),
      fl.Rule.create("if Ambient is BRIGHT then Power is LOW",
      engine)
      ]
      )
]
```

118

You can see in this code that the Defuzzifier is called `Centroid`. `FuzzyLite` provides different kinds of Fuzzifiers, as listed here. All you need to do is replace them in the previous code:

- `fl.Centroid()`
- `fl.LargestOfMaximum()`
- `fl.MeanOfMaximum()`
- `fl.SmallestOfMaximum()`
- `fl.WeightedAverage()`
- `fl.Weighted Sum()`

Takagi-Sugeno-Kang Fuzzy Inference System

Takagi-Sugeno-Kang Fuzzy Inference Systems are used to model complex non-linear systems. The entire process of applying a Fuzzy Operator and then Fuzzifying the inputs is the same as with the Mamdani approach. The only change comes in the output membership function, which is either linear or constant. This section looks at the TSK approach.

Whatever output membership function you get, you apply a weighted average method of Defuzzification and get the final crisp output. As you have seen, there are different implication operators—the Mamdani or Sugeno approach. Here's what the different operators are composed of:

- For AND operations in rulebase, you use T-Norm
- For OR operations in rulebase, you use T-Co-Norm
- For implication operations, you use T-Norm
- For aggregation operations, you use T-Co-Norm

Using the same example you saw in Mamdani FIS, you can see how the TSK method works (see Figure 3-24).

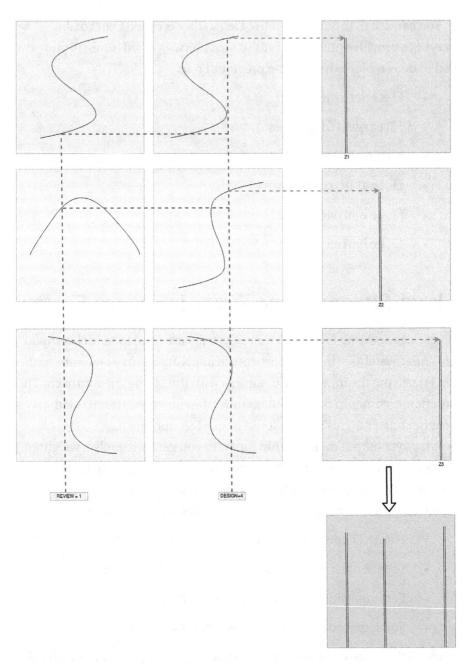

Figure 3-24. *The TSK method*

The diagram in Figure 3-24 represents the same Fuzzy If-Then rules you saw in Mamdani:

- If the product reviews are excellent or the product is beautiful, the product is recommended.

- If the product reviews are good or the product is nice, the product is somewhat recommended.

- If the product reviews are poor or the product is bad looking, the product is not recommended.

As mentioned, the TSK method uses the weighted average approach to find the Defuzzified crisp output. Therefore, using the following formula:

$$z^* = \frac{\sum_{i=1}^{n}\mu(x)*x_i}{\sum_{i=1}^{n}\mu(x)}$$

you get the final result as 13.3%.

You can use the FuzzyLite package to see the TSK application:

```
import fuzzylite as fl
#Declaring and Initializing the Fuzzy Engine
engine = fl.Engine(
    name="SimpleDimmer",
    description="Simple Dimmer Fuzzy System which dims light
    based upon Light Conditions"
)
#Defining the Input Variables (Fuzzification)
engine.input_variables = [
    fl.InputVariable(
    name="Ambient",
    description="",
    enabled=True,
```

```
    minimum=0.000,
    maximum=1.000,
    lock_range=False,
    terms=[
    fl.Triangle("DARK", 0.000, 0.250, 0.500), #Triangular
    Membership Function defining "Dark"
    fl.Triangle("MEDIUM", 0.250, 0.500, 0.750), #Triangular
    Membership Function defining "Medium"
    fl.Triangle("BRIGHT", 0.500, 0.750, 1.000) #Triangular
    Membership Function defining "Bright"
    ]
    )
]
#Defining the Output Variables (Defuzzification)
engine.output_variables = [
    fl.OutputVariable(
    name="Power",
    description="",
    enabled=True,
    minimum=0.000,
    maximum=1.000,
    lock_range=False,
    aggregation=None,
    defuzzifier=fl.WeightedAverage("TakagiSugeno"),
    lock_previous=False,
    terms=[
    fl.Constant("LOW", 0.250), #Constant Membership Function
    defining "LOW"
    fl.Constant("MEDIUM", 0.500), #Constant Membership
    Function defining "MEDIUM"
```

```
    fl.Constant("HIGH", 0.750) #Constant Membership Function
    defining "HIGH"
    ]
    )
]
#Creation of Fuzzy Rule Base
engine.rule_blocks = [
    fl.RuleBlock(
    name="",
    description="",
    enabled=True,
    conjunction=None,
    disjunction=None,
    implication=None,
    activation=fl.General(),
    rules=[
    fl.Rule.create("if Ambient is DARK then Power is HIGH",
    engine),
    fl.Rule.create("if Ambient is MEDIUM then Power is
    MEDIUM", engine),
    fl.Rule.create("if Ambient is BRIGHT then Power is LOW",
    engine)
    ]
    )
]
```

Tsukamoto Fuzzy Inference System

In Tsukamoto FIS, instead of having constant or linear output Fuzzy Membership, you have a monotonic membership function, which you Defuzzify using the weighted average approach. Figure 3-25 shows the Tsukamoto FIS process.

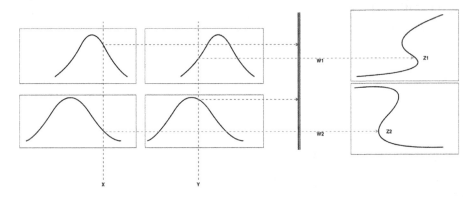

Figure 3-25. *The Tsukamoto method*

As you can see, the process remains the same, but the Defuzzification process changes. Therefore, the final result of this output will be given by the following formula:

$$Z = \frac{W_1 Z_1 + W_2 Z_2}{W_1 + W_2}$$

Since it is a weighted average approach, the process becomes very fast and hence time is not wasted during the detailed process of Defuzzification. The output of the Tsukamoto FIS is always crisp, no matter what the input types are.

The following sample code shows the application on Tsukamoto FIS in Python, using the FuzzyLite package:

```
import fuzzylite as fl
```

```
#Declaring and Initializing the Fuzzy Engine
engine = fl.Engine(
    name="SimpleDimmer",
    description="Simple Dimmer Fuzzy System which dims light
    based upon Light Conditions"
)
#Defining the Input Variables (Fuzzification)
engine.input_variables = [
    fl.InputVariable(
    name="Ambient",
    description="",
    enabled=True,
    minimum=0.000,
    maximum=1.000,
    lock_range=False,
    terms=[
    fl.Bell("Dark", -10.000, 5.000, 3.000), #Generalized Bell
    Membership Function defining "Dark"
    fl.Bell("medium", 0.000, 5.000, 3.000), #Generalized
    Bell  Membership Function defining "Medium"
    fl.Bell("Bright", 10.000, 5.000, 3.000) #Generalized
    Bell  Membership Function defining "Bright"
    ]
    )
]
#Defining the Output Variables (Defuzzification)
engine.output_variables = [
    fl.OutputVariable(
    name="Power",
    description="",
    enabled=True,
```

```
        minimum=0.000,
        maximum=1.000,
        lock_range=False,
        aggregation=fl.Maximum(),
        defuzzifier=fl.Centroid(200),
        lock_previous=False,
        terms=[
        fl.Sigmoid("LOW", 0.500, -30.000), #Triangular Membership
        Function defining "LOW Light"
        fl.Sigmoid("MEDIUM", 0.130, 30.000), #Triangular
        Membership Function defining "MEDIUM light"
        fl.Sigmoid("HIGH", 0.830, 30.000) #Triangular Membership
        Function defining "HIGH Light"
        fl.Triangle("HIGH", 0.500, 0.750, 1.000)
        ]
        )
]
#Creation of Fuzzy Rule Base
engine.rule_blocks = [
        fl.RuleBlock(
        name="",
        description="",
        enabled=True,
        conjunction=None,
        disjunction=None,
        implication=None,
        activation=fl.General(),
        rules=[
        fl.Rule.create("if Ambient is DARK then Power is HIGH",
        engine),
        fl.Rule.create("if Ambient is MEDIUM then Power is
        MEDIUM", engine),
```

```
fl.Rule.create("if Ambient is BRIGHT then Power is LOW",
engine)
]
)
]
```

Comparative Analysis of the Mamdani and TSK Fuzzy Inference System

The following list compares the two systems:

- Mamdani is not adaptable to any other algorithms, while TSK is adaptable.

- Mamdani uses the Defuzzification method for the evaluation of output, but TSK uses a weighted average method.

- When it comes to controlling the system with perfection, Mamdani does a good job in comparison to TSK.

- Mamdani has too many parameters as compared to TSK.

Summary

This chapter discussed the Fuzzy Inference Systems in detail. It first reviewed the different types of Defuzzifiers, with examples. Later, the chapter moved on to three Fuzzy Inference Systems: Mamdani, TSK, and Tsukamoto Fuzzy Inference Systems. You learned about the application of all the inference systems in Python using the Fuzzylite package.

The next chapter sets the foundation of Machine Learning, which will act as a base to understanding the concept of Fuzzy Neural Networks in the upcoming chapters.

CHAPTER 4

Introduction to Machine Learning

The previous chapter discussed different Fuzzy Inference Systems, which are used to make various practical control systems. But these systems are static, which means the fuzzification process, defuzzification process, defining memberships, etc. is all done manually. With intelligent systems, it is always better to learn most of the things from the data, rather than hard-coding it directly. This area of Fuzzy Inference Systems is where most of the parameters are learned. The neural networks approach is called Fuzzy Neural Networks.

This chapter sets the foundation of Machine Learning. You will learn about different concepts of Machine Learning that'll help you understand the core concepts of Fuzzy Neural Networks later in this book.

This chapter starts by giving an introduction to Machine Learning. You will learn about different types of problems that Machine Learning can solve and how to measure the effectiveness of various models. It covers how the data is represented and partitioned in Machine Learning and what the advantages of having these partitions are.

Machine Learning is a branch of Artificial Intelligence that involves the ability to learn from the data, continuously from experience, without having to explicitly program the parameters. Machine Learning learns from the data provided to it by applying different statistical and

© Himanshu Singh, Yunis Ahmad Lone 2020
H. Singh and Y. A. Lone, *Deep Neuro-Fuzzy Systems with Python*,
https://doi.org/10.1007/978-1-4842-5361-8_4

mathematical approaches. Machine Learning tries to determine the hidden patterns present inside the data. Based on these patterns, the model tries to predict something when new data is provided.

Machine Learning

Figure 4-1 illustrates the categories of Machine Learning. Classification Machine Learning (ML) models help you solve the problems when the output is categorical. A categorical output includes the variables that can be nominal or ordinal. For example, based on some specific traits, you ask your model to determine whether the stock price of a particular company is going to move up or down in the coming months. This is a classification problem.

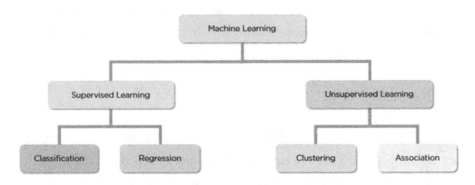

Figure 4-1. *Machine Learning algorithms*

Similarly, if you provide an image and want the ML model to classify whether the image is a person or an animal, this is again a classification problem. Conversely, instead of asking the ML model to classify the data, if you ask it to directly predict the output in the form of a numerical value, that's called a regression problem. For example, say you try to predict the price of a stock next month or the age of a person based on an image provided. This is a regression problem.

As discussed in the previous section, when an ML model tries to predict the category based on the data, that's a classification problem. An ML model can classify data into two classes or multiple classes. When you classify data into two classes, the ML problem is called a binary classification problem (see Figure 4-2). If there are more than two classes, it's called a multiclass classification problem.

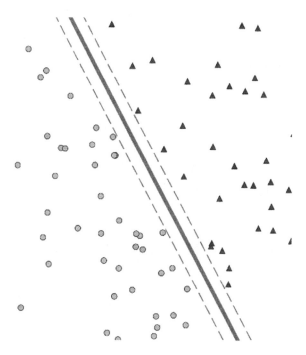

Figure 4-2. *Binary classification*

Classification Machine Learning Problems

The following are a few examples of binary and multiclass classification problems:

- Given an image, is it a cat or a dog—binary classification

- Whether a person will be able to pay their loan or not—binary classification

- Classifying an ECG signal to one of 13 health issues—multiclass classification

- A chatbot sending issues to different departments based on the question asked—multiclass classification

- Classifying different types of driver distractions—multiclass classification

Regression Machine Learning Problems

An ML model that tries to predict an actual numerical value based on the data is within the domain of a regression ML problem (see Figure 4-3). Here are some examples of regression problems:

- Predicting a stock market price

- Predicting a company's revenue in the next quarter

- Finding the optimal speed of a self-driving car

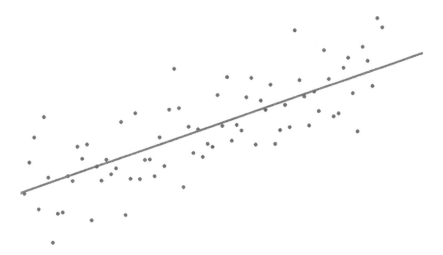

Figure 4-3. *Regression*

Whether they are classification or regression problems, an ML model always learns from experience. The next section explains what exactly is meant by *experience*.

The Experience

Experience for an ML model is simply the data that you give to it, from which it learns the hidden patterns and then solves a problem. Data given to the model is specific to the type of problem that you expect the model to solve. When you talk about learning from the data in relation to classification and regression problems, different features are present in it along with the feature that you want to predict or classify. For example, if you want to predict the stock price or classify the stock price movement, you may have data containing different features, such as information about high, low, open, and close to a specific stock. Past movement of the stock or past stock price information is also provided. So, the model looks at the entire dataset and then the actual value for that specific time. Based on that, it learns the relationship between all the variables. Once the learning

133

process is done and you provide new data, the model looks at all the new features, understands the relationship, and then tries to predict or classify the new data.

This value that you are predicting or classifying is called the *target variable* or *dependent variable* (say, Y). All the other variables are called *independent variables* (say, x). You can say that the target variable is a function of all the independent variables, as given here. The function can be linear or nonlinear. Figure 4-4 shows gradient descent graph, which is one of the learning algorithms.

$$Y = f(X)$$

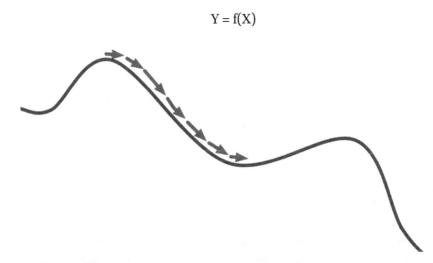

Figure 4-4. *Learning graph (gradient descent)*

In classification and regression problems, the data always contains a dependent variable, which is the variable that you want to predict or classify. There is one field of ML where the dependent variable is not given. These problems are the clustering or association types. Therefore, based on the data available, Machine Learning approaches fall into two areas:

- Supervised learning
- Unsupervised learning

Supervised and Unsupervised Learning

If you are crossing a road with the support of someone, this can be called a supervised approach. But, if you start crossing the road without anyone's help, it's an unsupervised approach. Taking a hint from this example, you can say that a supervised learning approach includes data that contains dependent variables. That's when the model looks at the input and output variables and tries to learn the relationship between them.

With unsupervised learning, the data doesn't contain the target variable (Y, as specified in supervised learning). It must look at the dataset and then find the similarities/differences/patterns between them. Based on that, you can have different unsupervised learning approaches. You have already seen the supervised learning approaches, which are classification and regression. Unsupervised learning approaches include clustering, decomposition, and association. Figure 4-5 represents both problem statements visually.

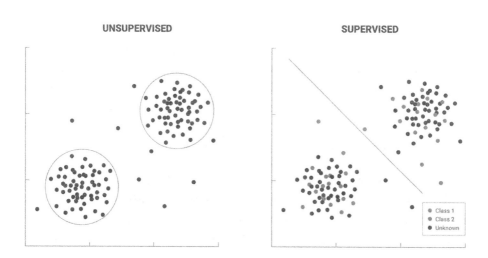

Figure 4-5. *Supervised versus unsupervised learning*

The following algorithms use supervised learning approaches:

- Linear/logistic regression

- K-nearest neighbor

- Naive Bayes theorem

- Decision trees

- Ensemble trees

- Support vector machines

- Neural networks

The following algorithms use unsupervised learning approaches:

- Hierarchical clustering

- K-means clustering

- Apriori rule

- Neural networks

Once you have decided what kind of problem your Machine Learning model needs to solve and select one of the algorithms from these lists, you come to the next phase, which is finding the performance of the model.

The Measure of Performance

Once your model is ready, it's time to ensure that you get accurate results. For that, you measure the performance of the model, based on the problem that it is trying to solve—classification or regression.

For Classification problems, the following are some of the measures you use:

- Accuracy

- Precision

- Recall or sensitivity
- F1-score
- Confusion matrix

For regression problems, here are some of the metrics:

- Root mean squared error
- AIC
- R2-score

The next sections discuss these measurements and metrics using the Titanic and House Price datasets.

Understanding Titanic and House Price Datasets

This section explains the accuracy measures using the two datasets available in the public domain—the Titanic and House Price datasets. You will use the Titanic dataset to learn about the classification measures and the House Price dataset for regression measures. You can download both datasets from Kaggle. Here are the links that you can follow for the downloads:

```
https://www.kaggle.com/c/titanic/data
https://www.kaggle.com/alphaepsilon/housing-prices-dataset
```

Remember, you'll need to register at kaggle.com to use these datasets. Assuming that the datasets have been downloaded, you'll start by understanding and exploring the Titanic dataset in Python. The Titanic dataset contains information about the people who survived the sinking of the Titanic, as well as the people who died. The main aim of this dataset is to help determine the likelihood of survival based on the information you report about a person (such as age, gender, class of ticket purchased, etc.). Let's look at the features in this dataset by loading it in Python.

```
#Reading data
import pandas as pd
data = pd.read_csv("train.csv")
data.head()
```

Once you execute this code, you'll get top five rows of the entire dataset, as shown in Figure 4-6.

	PassengerId	Survived	Pclass	Name	Sex	Age	SibSp	Parch	Ticket	Fare	Cabin	Embarked
0	1	0	3	Braund, Mr. Owen Harris	male	22.0	1	0	A/5 21171	7.2500	NaN	S
1	2	1	1	Cumings, Mrs. John Bradley (Florence Briggs Th...	female	38.0	1	0	PC 17599	71.2833	C85	C
2	3	1	3	Heikkinen, Miss. Laina	female	26.0	0	0	STON/O2. 3101282	7.9250	NaN	S
3	4	1	1	Futrelle, Mrs. Jacques Heath (Lily May Peel)	female	35.0	1	0	113803	53.1000	C123	S
4	5	0	3	Allen, Mr. William Henry	male	35.0	0	0	373450	8.0500	NaN	S

Figure 4-6. *Titanic dataset*

In total, there are 11 columns in this dataset. (A subset of an entire database is called a *dataset*.) Here's an explanation of the columns:

- Survived: 1 means the person survived, 0 means the person did not survive

- Pclass: Passenger's class

- Name: Passenger's name

- Sex: Passenger's sex

- Age: Passenger's age

- SibSp: Number of siblings/spouses aboard

- Parch: Number of parents/children aboard

- Ticket: Ticket number

- Fare: Amount paid for the tickets

- Cabin: Cabin

- Embarked: Port of embarkation

Since the dataset classifies whether a person survived the incident or not, Survived is the dependent variable. The others are independent variables. You will use this dataset for all the classification measures in the next section. Let's move on to the Housing Price dataset.

Using the House Price dataset (see Figure 4-7), you can predict the price of house based on different features. This dataset contains 81 columns, with SalePrice as the dependent variable. You can explore the dataset using the following Python statements:

```
#Reading data
import pandas as pd
data = pd.read_csv("train_hp.csv")
data.head()
```

LotArea	Street	Alley	LotShape	LandContour	Utilities	...	PoolArea	PoolQC	Fence	MiscFeature	MiscVal	MoSold	YrSold	Sale Type	SaleCondition	SalePri
8450	Pave	NaN	Reg	Lvl	AllPub	...	0	NaN	NaN	NaN	0	2	2008	WD	Normal	2085
9600	Pave	NaN	Reg	Lvl	AllPub	...	0	NaN	NaN	NaN	0	5	2007	WD	Normal	1815
11250	Pave	NaN	IR1	Lvl	AllPub	...	0	NaN	NaN	NaN	0	9	2008	WD	Normal	2235
9550	Pave	NaN	IR1	Lvl	AllPub	...	0	NaN	NaN	NaN	0	2	2006	WD	Abnorml	140C
14260	Pave	NaN	IR1	Lvl	AllPub	...	0	NaN	NaN	NaN	0	12	2008	WD	Normal	250C

Figure 4-7. *House Price dataset*

This example uses the 80 columns to predict the target variable, SalePrice. Before moving to the measures, you must also understand the different types of splits in data.

Different Types of Data (Datasets)

Machine Learning generally has three types of datasets (see Figure 4-8):

- Training set
- Validation set
- Test set

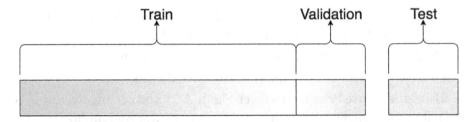

Figure 4-8. *Dataset partition*

You'll get the entire database as one single file. It can be in any format, including CSV, XLSX, SQL, etc. This example divides this data into three parts. The training set consists of the data with which the model learns. The validation set is where you test the performance of the model. The main data is also split into two parts. The first part contains most of the data and is called the training set and the remaining data is the validation set. The test set is totally unseen data. This is where you accept or reject the model. This is similar to the validation set, but the data is not a part of the training set. It's a totally new set of data that you get from the new source.

The next section discusses different types of performance measures. Later sections will discuss these sets more as well.

Classification Problems: Measures

Confusion Matrix

Once you apply the model to the test data, you get the confusion matrix, by which you can determine the performance of the model. In the Titanic dataset, you have a binary classification problem, whereby you want to classify whether a person survived or not. The confusion matrix in that case will look like Figure 4-9.

n=165	Predicted: NO	Predicted: YES
Actual: NO	50	10
Actual: YES	5	100

Figure 4-9. *Confusion matrix*

In a binary confusion matrix, you have two rows and two columns. Rows contain the actual values present in the test data, while columns contain the predicted value of the model. You can then determine how many times the model predicted the right results and how many times the wrong results were predicted.

There are 50 instances where NO was predicted and the actual value was also NO. There are 100 instances where YES was predicted and the actual data was YES. But there are also 10 instances where the predicted was YES and the actual data was NO, as well as 5 instances where the predicted data was NO and the actual data was YES. Therefore, you can say that most of the time, the model gives accurate results, but there are chances of errors. If you quantify the table, you come to different accuracy measures. But, before moving to those metrics, you first need to understand the different terminologies related to the confusion matrix.

- True Positives: If it's actually YES, how often the model predicts YES.

- True Negatives: If it's actually NO, how often the model predicts YES.

- False Positives (Type I Error): If it's actually NO, how often the model predicts NO.

- False Negatives (Type II Error): If it's actually YES, how often the model predicts NO.

Accuracy

This is the overall accuracy of the model. It's determined using this formula:

$$accuracy = \frac{True\ Positive + True\ Negative}{True\ Positive + False\ Positive + True\ Negative + False\ Negative}$$

True Negative Rate

TNR represents the negatives that are correctly classified. It is also called the specificity of the model. You can get the True Negative Rate of a model by using this formula:

$$specificity = \frac{True\ Negative}{False\ Positive + True\ Negative}$$

Recall or True Positive Rate

If you want to know how many instances have been misclassified as false negatives, then you are looking for recall. It is also called the true positive rate or sensitivity. You can get the recall of a model by using the formula:

$$recall = \frac{True\ Positive}{True\ Positive + False\ Negative}$$

Precision

If you want to know how many instances have been misclassified as false positives, you are looking for precision. You can get the precision of a model by using the formula:

$$precision = \frac{True\ Positive}{True\ Positive + False\ Positive}$$

F1-Score

When you take the weighted average of recall and precision, it's called the F1-score. It reflects the model's accuracy, considering both precision and recall.

$$f1 = \frac{2 * Precision * Recall}{\left(Precision + Recall \right)}$$

ROC Curve

When you plot the true positive rates of the model with the false positive rate, in order to visualize the model summary, it is called the ROC curve (see Figure 4-10).

AUC: 0.809

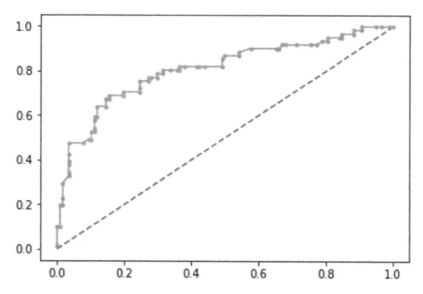

Figure 4-10. *ROC curve*

You can plot this diagram at different classification thresholds. The higher the area under the curve, the better the model. To better understand all these concepts, let's apply them to the Titanic dataset. This example uses Logistic Regression as an example model to test accuracy.

```
#Reading data
import pandas as pd
data = pd.read_csv("train_hp.csv")

#Splitting Data into Categorical and Numerical Dataframes
import numpy as np
data_cat = data.select_dtypes(include=[object])
data_num = data.select_dtypes(include=np.number)

#Checking the number of null values
data_cat.isnull().sum()
```

```
Name            0
Sex             0
Ticket          0
Cabin         687
Embarked        2
dtype: int64
```

```
data_num.isnull().sum()
```

```
PassengerId     0
Survived        0
Pclass          0
Age           177
SibSp           0
Parch           0
Fare            0
dtype: int64
```

```
#Dropping the Columns having null values and columns which are
not important
data_cat.drop(["Cabin","Embarked","Name","Ticket"], axis=1,
inplace=True)
data_num.drop(["Age","PassengerId"], axis=1, inplace=True)

#Checking the null values again
data_cat.isnull().sum()
```

```
Sex      0
dtype: int64
```

```
data_num.isnull().sum()
```

```
Survived    0
Pclass      0
SibSp       0
Parch       0
Fare        0
dtype: int64
```

```
#Converting categorical variables into numbers
from sklearn.preprocessing import LabelEncoder
le = LabelEncoder()
data_cat = data_cat.apply(le.fit_transform)

#Combining both dataframes
data = pd.concat([data_cat,data_num], axis=1)

#Defining dependent and independent variables
X = data.drop(["Survived"], axis=1)
Y = pd.DataFrame(data[["Survived"]])
```

```
#Defining data into train and test set
from sklearn.model_selection import train_test_split
X_train, X_test, y_train, y_test = train_test_split(X, Y, test_
size=0.20)
```

```
#Applying Logistic Regression
from sklearn.linear_model import LogisticRegression
lr = LogisticRegression()
lr.fit(X_train,y_train)
```

```
#Predicting Values
pred = lr.predict(X_test)
```

```
#Finding different classification measures
from sklearn.metrics import confusion_matrix, accuracy_score,
recall_score, precision_score, f1_score
confusion_matrix(pred,y_test)
```

```
array([[100,  19],
       [ 18,  42]], dtype=int64)
```

```
accuracy_score(pred,y_test)
```

```
0.7932960893854749
```

```
recall_score(pred,y_test)
```

```
0.7
```

```
precision_score(pred,y_test)
```

```
0.6885245901639344
```

```
f1_score(pred,y_test)
```

```
0.6942148760330578
```

```
from sklearn.metrics import roc_auc_score, roc_curve
from matplotlib import pyplot
# predict probabilities
probs = lr.predict_proba(X_test)
# keep probabilities for the positive outcome only
probs = probs[:, 1]
# calculate AUC
auc = roc_auc_score(y_test, probs)
print('AUC: %.3f' % auc)
# calculate roc curve
fpr, tpr, thresholds = roc_curve(y_test, probs)
# plot no skill
pyplot.plot([0, 1], [0, 1], linestyle='--')
# plot the roc curve for the model
pyplot.plot(fpr, tpr, marker='.')
# show the plot
pyplot.show()
```

So, you can see from the code that:

- The accuracy was 79%

- The precision was 68.8%

- The recall was 70%

- The F1-score was 69%

- The area under the curve was 80.9%

You can now use other Machine Learning algorithms to see if they give better results than Logistic Regression.

Regression Problems

Now that you understand the metrics for classification models, it's time to look at the regression model performance metrics.

Root Mean Squared Error

Root Mean Squared (RMS) Error is given by this formula:

$$error = \sqrt{\frac{\sum_{i=1}^{n}\left(\hat{y}-y\right)^2}{n}}$$

Using this formula, you get the error of the model. The smaller the error, the better the model. $\hat{y}$ is the predicted value while y is the original value. n is the total number of observations.

R-Squared Summary

This measure indicates how close the data is to the predicted regression line. This model explains the variation in the dependent variable. This information is given by R Squared Summary. It can be stated using the following formula:

$$R^2 = \frac{Explained\ variation}{Total\ variation}$$

Mathematically, R^2 can be represented as follows:

$$R^2 = 1 - \frac{SS_{residual}}{SS_{total}}$$

where:

$$SS_{residual} = \sum_{i}^{n} e_i^2 \ \text{ and }\ SS_{total} = \sum_{i}^{n}\left(y_i - \underline{y}\right)^2$$

The value of R-squared is always between 0 and 100%:

- 0% means that the model is not able to explain any variance present in the data.

- 100% means that the model is able to explain all the variance present in the data.

Adjusted R-Squared Summary

The R^2 score has a fault in that it assumes every independent variable affects the dependent variable. In real life, this may not be the case. Therefore, adjusted R^2 takes only those variables into consideration that actually have some effect on the dependent variable. It is represented by the following formula:

$$adjR^2 = 1 - \frac{(1 - R^2)(n - 1)}{n - k - 1}$$

Akaike Information Criteria

If you know the Root Mean Squared Error of the model, the square of it will give you the Mean Squared Error. Using it, you can find the AIC of the model, as given here:

$$AIC = nlog(MSE) + 2k$$

Where MSE is the Mean Squared Error, n is the total number of observations, and k is the number of regression coefficients, which can be called independent variables.

People use the AIC score because sometimes when you try to add new parameters inside the model, the chances of overfitting increases. AIC tries to solve this problem by introducing a penalty for the number of parameters inside the model.

Bayesian Information Criteria

Bayesian Information Criteria (BIC) is similar to AIC, but the strength of penalty is greater. It can be represented by the following formula:

$$BIC = k * log(n) - 2 * log(L(\theta))$$

$L(\theta)$ represents the likelihood of the model tested.

Let's apply all the measures to the Housing Price dataset. This example uses linear regression to understand the applications.

```
#Reading Data
import pandas as pd
house_price = pd.read_csv("train_hp.csv")
```

```
#Partition into Categorical and Numerical Variables
import numpy as np
cat = house_price.select_dtypes(include=[object])
num = house_price.select_dtypes(include=[np.number])
```

```
#Checking Null Values
cat.isnull().sum()
num.isnull().sum()
```

```
#Removing unnecessary columns
cat.drop(["Alley", "PoolQC", "Fence", "MiscFeature"], axis=1,
inplace=True)
```

```
#Removing Categorical Null Values with Mode
cat.BsmtCond.value_counts().idxmax() cat.BsmtCond.fillna(cat.
BsmtCond.value_counts().idxmax(),inplace=True)
cat.BsmtQual.fillna(cat.BsmtQual.value_counts().
idxmax(),inplace=True)
```

```
cat.BsmtExposure.fillna(cat.BsmtExposure.value_counts().
idxmax(),inplace=True)
cat.BsmtFinType1.fillna(cat.BsmtFinType1.value_counts().
idxmax(),inplace=True)
cat.BsmtFinType2.fillna(cat.BsmtFinType2.value_counts().
idxmax(),inplace=True)
cat.FireplaceQu.fillna(cat.FireplaceQu.value_counts().
idxmax(),inplace=True)
cat.GarageCond.fillna(cat.GarageCond.value_counts().
idxmax(),inplace=True)
cat.GarageFinish.fillna(cat.GarageFinish.value_counts().
idxmax(),inplace=True)
cat.GarageQual.fillna(cat.GarageQual.value_counts().
idxmax(),inplace=True)
cat.GarageType.fillna(cat.GarageType.value_counts().
idxmax(),inplace=True)
cat.Electrical.fillna(cat.Electrical.value_counts().
idxmax(),inplace=True)
cat.MasVnrType.fillna(cat.MasVnrType.value_counts().
idxmax(),inplace=True)

#Removing Numerical Null Values with Mean
num.LotFrontage.fillna(num.LotFrontage.mean(),inplace=True)
num.GarageYrBlt.fillna(num.GarageYrBlt.mean(),inplace=True)
num.MasVnrArea.fillna(num.MasVnrArea.mean(),inplace=True)

#Converting words to Integers
from sklearn.preprocessing import LabelEncoder
le = LabelEncoder()
cat1 = cat.apply(le.fit_transform)

#Combining two dataframes
house_price2 = pd.concat([cat1, num], axis=1)
```

```
#Getting Dependent and Independent Variables
X = house_price2.drop(["SalePrice"], axis=1)
Y = pd.DataFrame(house_price2["SalePrice"])

#Getting Train and Test Set
from sklearn.model_selection import train_test_split
X_train, X_test, Y_train, Y_test = train_test_split(X, Y, test_
size=0.20)

#Applying Linear Regression
import statsmodels.api as sm
est = sm.OLS(Y_train, X_train)
est2 = est.fit()
est2.summary()
```

You can see in Figure 4-11 that, with summary(), you can see all the measures. There are various other Python packages that provide these measures explicitly.

OLS Regression Results

Dep. Variable:	SalePrice	R-squared:	0.974
Model:	OLS	Adj. R-squared:	0.973
Method:	Least Squares	F-statistic:	569.3
Date:	Wed, 04 Sep 2019	Prob (F-statistic):	0.00
Time:	16:05:42	Log-Likelihood:	-13758.
No. Observations:	1168	AIC:	2.766e+04
Df Residuals:	1095	BIC:	2.803e+04
Df Model:	73		
Covariance Type:	nonrobust		

Figure 4-11. *Numerical measures*

Overfitting versus Underfitting

The next chapter looks at some of these Machine Learning approaches, but before that, you must be able to determine if your model is giving you poor performance. This can either be due to *overfitting* or *underfitting* of the data.

The data that you get to make the model is only a sample of all the data present in the universe. You can say that the data is incomplete and noisy. That's why, when you train the model, it tries to learn how well it is generalizing to new data. In other words, you can say that whatever the model has learned, whether it is able to apply these concepts to new data successfully is referred to as *generalization*.

If the model is applied to the data a little too well, it is called an *overfitting problem*. Sometimes there are too many details present in the data and a lot of unnecessary information is also present. If the model learns from this highly specific data, especially the details and the extra noise, it could lead to overfitting. This negatively impacts the performance. In underfitting, the model is not able to learn from the data, so it can't perform well on the new unseen data.

Underfitting and overfitting happen when you have imbalanced datasets. Suppose for a binary classification problem, you have 90% of the data from one category and the remaining from the other. In this case, the model will learn most of the things related to the first category and very little related to the second category. This can also happen if you train the model a little too vigorously or add parameters to the model.

Overfitting happens when you train the model a little too long, while underfitting happens when the model is not trained long enough. In other words, you can say that if you train the model to such an extent where error starts to increase, overfitting may happen. But, if you stop training the model when the error is high and can still be reduced, underfitting may happen.

The best approach to solve this issue is to find the perfect spot between overfitting and underfitting. Figure 4-12 shows this best method. This concept is called a *bias-variance tradeoff,* and it's explained in the next section.

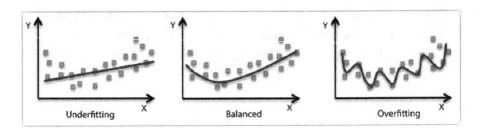

Figure 4-12. *Overfitting vs. underfitting*

Bias and Variance

When a model is trained by giving very little attention to the training data, then it becomes a biased model. In this scenario, the difference between the prediction and the original value becomes quite high. In other words, the error is large.

When overfitting happens in the model, that is when a lot of attention is given to the data, including the noise and the details. The variance of the model becomes high. Therefore, in this scenario, the model performs really well in the training data but not on the unseen data.

To solve these problems, you use the concept of a *Bias-Variance Tradeoff.* In this scenario, you try to find a middle approach where neither the bias nor the variance is high. In other words, you try to avoid both overfitting and underfitting in the data. Figure 4-13 shows how bias and variance are related to the concepts of overfitting and underfitting.

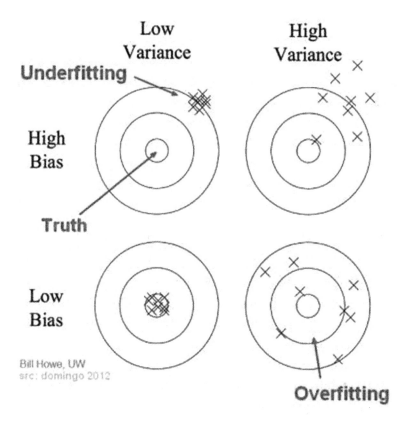

Figure 4-13. *Bias and variance*

Here are some approaches that can be used to solve the problem of overfitting.

- Adding cross-validations

- Training with more data

- Removing features

- Early stopping of training

- Adding regularizations

- Using the concept of ensembling

You can solve the problem of underfitting by:

- Adding features

- Training with more data

- Increasing the training time

- Removing regularizations

Summary

This chapter looked at the basic knowledge required to understand Machine Learning, as well as Fuzzy Neural Network architectures. It discussed supervised and unsupervised learning methods, and Machine Learning applications in classification and regression problems. The chapter also discussed different accuracy measures for both problems and how they are applied in Python.

The next chapter discusses some of these Machine Learning algorithms in detail. You will learn how to apply most of the concepts discussed in this chapter there.

CHAPTER 5

Artificial Neural Networks

The previous chapter discussed various terminology related to Machine Learning and some of the metrics used to check the accuracy of the model. This chapter discusses the concepts of neural networks.

This chapter begins by explaining artificial neural networks and their components. It covers some of these components in detail, like activation functions, layers, etc. It then covers some of the advanced architectures of neural networks, like convolutional neural networks, recurrent neural networks, long short-term memory, and gated recurrent units. It also shows some applications of these concepts in Python.

Artificial Neural Networks Primer

Artificial neural networks (ANNs) are inspired by the functioning of biological neurons. Core Machine Learning algorithms use statistical concepts to learn different patterns present in the data. ANNs try to mimic human brain and neurons as much as possible to learn patterns. By using the mathematical techniques of linear algebra and calculus, ANNs learn from the data and try to find patterns.

© Himanshu Singh, Yunis Ahmad Lone 2020
H. Singh and Y. A. Lone, *Deep Neuro-Fuzzy Systems with Python*,
https://doi.org/10.1007/978-1-4842-5361-8_5

An ANN consists of the following layers:

- Input layer
- Hidden layer
- Output layer

The input layer contains the examples with which you want to train the network. All the data you have, with which you want to make the system learn, is provided to the input layer. Training the network means that the machine tries to find all the possible patterns present in the data and then learn it. The benefit of training is that when you give a new set of data, the machine tries to apply the learned patterns to the new set. If the patterns match, a decision is made based on what was done to the training data following this pattern.

Hidden layers try to look at different combinations of the input layer and decide which of them is important, and how much importance should be given to them. They do this with the help of weights. Therefore, you can say that the hidden layers take weighted input.

Once all the processing is done, the output layer computes all the outputs of the program and provides the results. Figure 5-1 shows the basic representation of all three layers.

Neural networks operate by applying the concepts of forward and backpropagation. Therefore, it is imperative that you understand these concepts before moving on to ANN architectures in detail.

The graph in Figure 5-1 is also called a computational graph. Each node in the graph is represented by a circle and represents a variable. This variable can be a scalar, vector, or tensor. Sometimes it can also be another variable. Each node is computed by applying some operation on the previous node. Therefore, in Figure 5-1, the hidden nodes are computed from input nodes and the output nodes are computed from the hidden nodes. This process where the output node is computed by the operations of previous nodes and the information provided from the input nodes are passed right to the output node is called *forward propagation*.

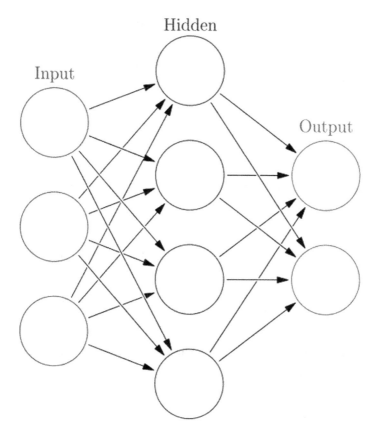

Figure 5-1. *Computational graph of ANNs*

Once the output nodes are created and their values are computed using the forward propagation approach, there is a need to compute the gradient, which requires the information to flow backward from the output node to input node. This concept is called *backpropagation*. In neural networks, it becomes very important to calculate gradients using the backpropagation approach because it helps minimize the cost function, which leads to much better and more accurate predictions.

Mathematically, the process of backpropagation can be represented by:

$$\Delta_x f(x, y)$$

You can calculate the gradient of a function f(), where x is the set of variables whose derivatives are required and y are the variables whose derivatives are not required (for example, input nodes). In learning algorithms like neural networks, this output function is called a *cost function*, and it's represented by:

$$J(\theta)$$

For a binary classification problem, the loss function $J(\theta)$ can be defined as follows:

$$J(\theta) = -\frac{1}{N} \sum_{i=1}^{N} y * log(p(y)) + (1-y) * log(p(1-y))$$

So this equation is differentiated with respect to the input nodes, until the time when the loss value is minimum. This minimum value is known by reaching a minimum point, called the global minima, in the gradient descent process. Figure 5-2 shows the gradient descent process.

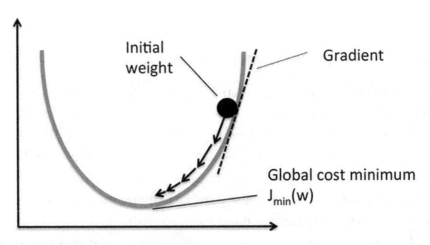

Figure 5-2. *Gradient descent*

Every time you differentiate the cost function to find the gradients, you move down the parabolic curve shown in Figure 5-2. The aim of backpropagation is to reach a point at the bottom of the curve where the value of the loss function is at a minimum. As the value becomes minimum, you find the values of variables that gave that value. In the case of neural networks, these variables are called *weights* and *bias*. You use these variables to predict the next set of values in the test set.

Keeping these concepts in mind, it's time to dive deeper into ANNs. ANNs can be classified into two types:

- Perceptrons

- Multi-layer ANNs

The next sections explain these two ANNs and then the chapter moves forward to explain some of the complex neural network architectures used in the domain of computer vision and natural language processing.

Perceptrons

A *perceptron* is a single-layered neural network, which means it only has the input layer. Using different parameters, you can get the output. Its architecture may look like Figure 5-3.

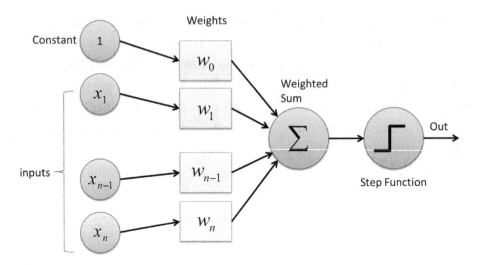

Figure 5-3. *Typical perceptron architecture*

Perceptron is mainly used as a linear (binary) classifier. A binary classifier classifies the input into only two categories. A perceptron consists of the following parts, as depicted in Figure 5-3:

- Input layer

- Weights and bias parameters

- Summation of weighted inputs

- Applying activation/step function on the weighted sum to get the output

So, in a perceptron, all the inputs are multiplied with the learned weights (w). These weights are learned through the process of backpropagation. The summation of the weighted input takes place and the output is passed to the activation function, which provides the final output. There are different types of activation functions, which give different outputs based on the formula. To get a binary classification, you use the sigmoid or ReLU activation functions. Before you move further to multi-layered perceptrons, take a look at activation functions.

Activation Functions

Each neuron in the hidden layer or output layer has its own activation function. This helps to decide whether the output from a particular neuron is important or not. The weights that the system has learned are multiplied with the input neuron value. Then, a bias value is added. The output value is based on the activation function, which determines the importance. When you have an activation function in the output neuron, it takes the output of all the previous neurons, where activation function is applied, and gives a final answer by performing the weighted sum. There are different types of activation functions, some of which are:

- Sigmoid

- Tanh

- Softmax

- ReLU

- Leaky ReLU

Sigmoid Activation Function

A sigmoid activation function has an s-shaped curve. Its range lies from 0 to 1. Since its upper and lower limit is 0 and 1, it is most widely used with binary classification problems. Here is the formula and the curve of the sigmoid activation function (see Figure 5-4), followed by the Python implementation.

$$Sigmoid(x) = \frac{1}{1 + e^{-x}}$$

```
import numpy as np
def sigmoid(x):
      return 1 / (1 + np.exp(-x))
```

163

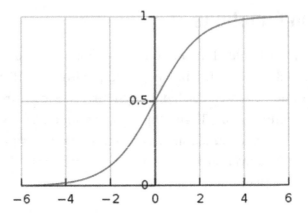

Figure 5-4. *Sigmoid activation function*

Tanh Activation Function

Tanh is also referred to as the hyperbolic tangent function. The shape of this function is also like an s, but its limit is from -1 to +1. This function is used when you want to consider negative outputs. Generally, in the hidden layers using Tanh is recommended because it allows the output of different layers to give negative values as well. Outputs of the output layer can be given to the sigmoid function to get positive values, but in the middle layers, more information should be captured from the data and Tanh provides you with a way to do that. Here is the formula and curve of the Tanh activation function (see Figure 5-5), followed by the Python implementation.

$$tanh(x) = \frac{2}{1+e^{-2x}}$$

```
import numpy as np
def tanh(x):
        return np.tanh(x)
```

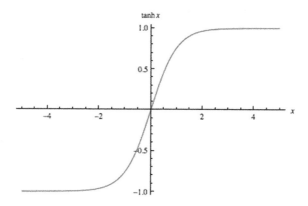

Figure 5-5. *Tanh activation function*

Softmax Activation Function

When you have binary classification problems, you use sigmoid functions. But if you have multiple classes, you should use softmax activation functions instead. The output of a softmax function is the probability of each class, concerning all the classes. The class with the maximum probability is considered the predicted class. Here is the formula and curve of a softmax function (see Figure 5-6), followed by the Python implementation.

$$softmax(x) = \frac{e^i}{\Sigma\, e^i}$$

```
import numpy as np
def softmax(x):
    exps = np.exp(x)
    return exps / np.sum(exps, axis=1).reshape(-1,1)
```

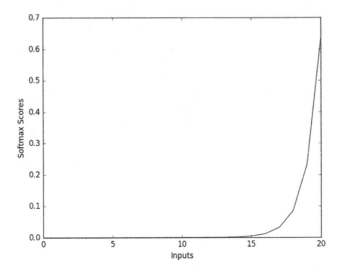

Figure 5-6. *Softmax activation function*

Rectified Linear Unit (ReLU) Activation Function

ReLU activation functions have a lower limit of 0, but no upper limit. This means that if the weighted sum is an integer or whole number, the exact value will be returned as output. But if the output is less than 0, the output will be converted into 0. It can be represented by the following formula and curve in Figure 5-7.

$$ReLU(x) = max(0, x)$$

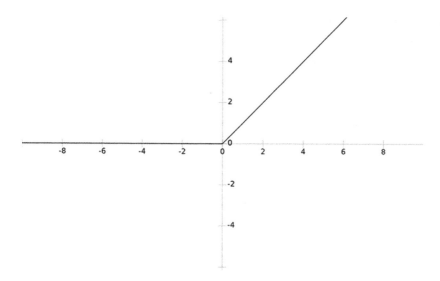

Figure 5-7. *ReLU activation function*

The following is the Python implementation.

```
import numpy as np
def relu(x):
        return 1.0*(x>0)
```

Leaky ReLU Activation Functions

This is exactly same as ReLU, but instead of having a lower limit as exactly 0, the values can be less than 0 so that the "dying ReLU problem" (discussed next) can be solved. You take a value α and multiply it by the original value so that the new value can be less than 0. Here is the formula and curve of leaky ReLU (see Figure 5-8), followed by the Python implementation.

$$LeakyReLU(x) = \{x, if\ x > 0\}$$

$$\{\alpha x, otherwise\}$$

167

```
import numpy as np
def leaky_relu(x, leaky_slope):
     d=np.zeros_like(x)
     d[X<=0]= leaky_slope
     d[X>0]=1
     return d
```

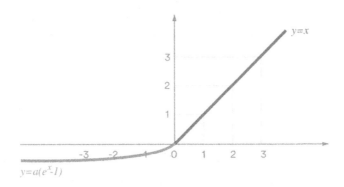

Figure 5-8. *Leaky ReLU activation function*

Here's the application of these Python methods:

```
import numpy as np

#Defining dummy values of x
x = np.linspace(-np.pi, np.pi, 12)

#Finding the Activation Function Outputs
sigmoid_output = sigmoid(x)
tanh_output = tanh(x)
softmax_output = softmax(x)
relu_output = relu(x)
leaky_relu_output = leaky_relu(x)

#Printing the Outputs
print(sigmoid_output)
```

```
print(tanh_output)
print(softmax_output)
print(relu_output)
print(leaky_relu_output)
```

What Is the Dying ReLU Problem?

Once the system has learned the weights and the bias of each neuron, and you give ReLU as an activation function, it usually gives the same output as it received as the input. But since any values that are less than 0 are converted to 0, the neurons may not be able to differentiate between the inputs. This problem is called the dying ReLU problem.

This makes a neuron practically dead. Even the slope of negative values is zero. If you keep moving forward and don't heed this problem, eventually a large part of the neural network will end up doing nothing. This problem generally happens when the learning rate is too high. By making the learning rate smaller or changing the activation function, for example to leaky- ReLU, you can solve the problem.

Multi-Layer ANNs

There are different types of multi-layer artificial neural networks. This chapter discusses the most relevant ones. The general architecture of a multi-layer ANN is shown in Figure 5-9.

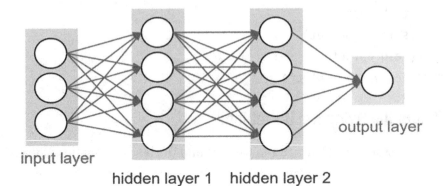

Figure 5-9. *Typical multi-layered ANN architecture*

The following sections review these ANNs:

- Convolutional neural networks

- Recurrent neural networks

- Long short-term memory

- Gated recurrent units

Convolutional Neural Networks

Convolutional neural networks are used in areas like image recognition, image classification, object detection, face recognition, etc. Before looking at the architecture and the process involved in a CNN, you should first understand how a computer looks and understands an image.

Computers break an image into a matrix of pixels and store the color code for each pixel, as you can see in Figure 5-10.

25	2	1	44
223	7	6	60
196	8	2	148
249	1	3	40
60	7	1	154
59	1	7	213
214	7	3	163
89	182	219	13
74	146	113	72
89	18	244	85
1	4	8	97
3	4	2	121
2	1	2	131
7	6	8	47
3	5	5	126
7	6	8	121
5	3	1	237

Figure 5-10. *Pixel matrix*

In the image in Figure 5-10, 1 represents white and 256 represents the darkest shade. It is not recommended to use normal neural networks when it comes to image processing. The more pixels there are, the more weights there are. This means if you have an RGB image that's 64x64, the number of pixels will be 12,288, and hence the number of weights will also be 12,288. There are images above 1000x800. Hence, even after a lot of computations, you will not get good accuracy. The solution for this is CNN. Instead of analyzing the entire input, CNN looks at a small part of it.

CNN image classifications take an input image (animal images, in this case), process it, and classify it under certain categories (e.g., dog, cat, or tiger). There are four basic components that define a basic convolutional network.

- The convolutional layer

- The activation function layer

- The pooling layer

- The output layer

Let's look at each of these in a little more detail.

The Convolutional Layer

The convolution layer is the main building block of a convolutional neural network. The convolution layer is used to understand the patterns present in the image and extract the interesting features from them. The total number of convolutional layers defines the total number of features that you want to extract from the image. For example, five convolutional layers means that five features are learned from an image. These features can be decipherable, like finding the edges or the threshold image, etc. or it they may be too complex for a human to understand. Hence, this is the main layer responsible for learning features, such as what unique features an image containing a human has and how they are different from the features present in an image of an animal. The values of all the filters are learnable, which means you must provide the matrix dimensions to a CNN, and it will automatically learn the best values for the convolution. This matrix of convolution is also called a kernel or filter.

Mathematically, each kernel operation happens in a way represented in Figure 5-11.

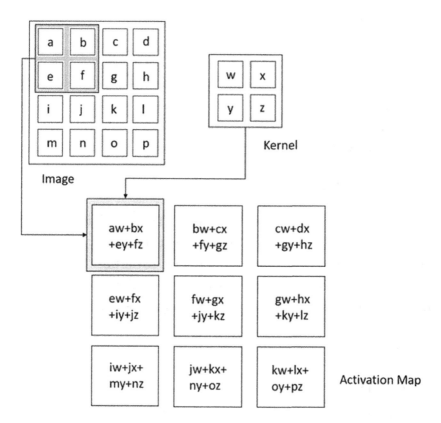

Figure 5-11. *Process of convolving through filters*

Based on the size of the kernel matrix, a matrix dot product happens at a specific portion of the image. This operation is continued until the kernel covers the entire image. This results in a new image with a smaller number of dimensions, as compared to the original image, but the depth of image is higher. The output is called an activation map and the process is called strides.

Padding

The filter might fit inside the image perfectly. But if it does not, you use the concept of padding. In this process, you add a few extra values in the input image so that the filter fits in well. The most commonly used value is 0 (called zero-padding). Alternatively, you can drop the part of the image where the filter doesn't fit.

Activation Function

The actual decision of classification is taken in this layer. The most used activation function in CNN is ReLU, the rectified linear unit. This helps the neurons give exact pixel values as output for all the positive values, but for all the negative values the output is always zero. This results in sparse matrix generation and hence means lesser computation time with better learning. Generally, pixel values are positive, so the problem of dying ReLU doesn't apply.

Pooling Layer

If an image is taken from a DSLR camera, the resolution will be very high. Since the resolution is high, the number of pixels will be high. Even though you use filters with a smaller dimension than the input image, the computational time will still be long. Therefore, to overcome this issue, you can use pooling. It is used to reduce the size of the input image, as well as the outcomes of convolutions. Because of this, the number of parameters that need to be analyzed is smaller. Hence, the computational time decreases. This layer operates on each feature map (the outcome of individual convolutions) independently.

Pooling, also called subsampling or downsampling, can be of different types:

- Max pooling

- Average pooling

- Sum pooling

The most common pooling approach is *max pooling*. Max pooling takes the largest element from the convolved matrix. Instead of the maximum, if you find the average number, it's called average pooling. Summing all elements in the convolved matrix is called sum pooling.

An example of the max pooling operation is shown in Figure 5-12.

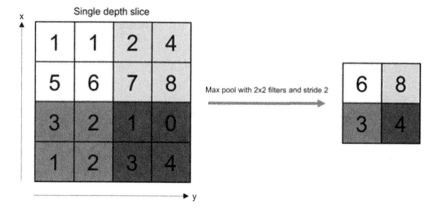

Figure 5-12. *Max pooling operation*

The Output Layer

After the processes of pooling and convolution are finished, the last layer operation starts, and the layer is called the output layer. The output layer is a network of fully connected layers, which means all the neurons in the previous layer are connected to all the neurons in the output layer. In the output layer, the normal operation of a neural network begins.

This means that once all the features are learned and extracted from multiple images, using the convolution and pooling operations, these learned features are passed to a regular neural network, which finally classifies the images using that information.

Figure 5-13 shows the entire operation of convolutional neural networks.

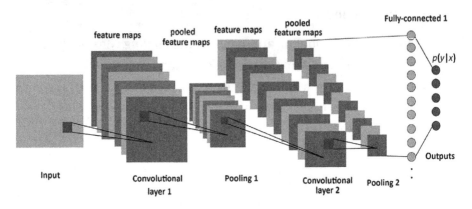

Figure 5-13. *Typical architecture of a CNN*

The following is the implementation of CNN on digits recognition applied to a MNIST dataset. You can find the segregated version of this code in the GitHub repository.

```python
from keras.datasets import mnist
import matplotlib.pyplot as plt
from keras.models import Sequential
from keras.layers import Dense, Conv2D, Flatten
from keras.utils import to_categorical

#download mnist data and split into train and test sets
(X_train, y_train), (X_test, y_test) = mnist.load_data()

f1 = plt.figure(1)
plt.imshow(X_train[0])
f2 = plt.figure(2)
```

```
plt.imshow(X_train[1])
plt.show()

#check image shape and data count
print(X_train[0].shape, len(X_train))
print(X_train[0].shape, len(X_test))

#reshape data to fit model
X_train = X_train.reshape(len(X_train),28,28,1)
X_test = X_test.reshape(len(X_test),28,28,1)

#One-hot encode target column
y_train = to_categorical(y_train)
y_test = to_categorical(y_test)
y_train[0]

#Create model
model = Sequential()

#Add Input CNN Layer
model.add(Conv2D(64, kernel_size=3, activation='relu', input_
shape=(28,28,1)))

#Add second CNN Layer
model.add(Conv2D(32, kernel_size=3, activation='relu'))

#Add the fully connected layer
model.add(Flatten())
model.add(Dense(10, activation='softmax'))

#Compile model using accuracy to measure model performance
model.compile(optimizer='adam', loss='categorical_
crossentropy', metrics=['accuracy'])

#Train the model
model.fit(X_train, y_train, validation_data=(X_test, y_test),
epochs=3)
```

```
#predict first 6 images in the test set
model.predict(X_test[:6])
```

```
#actual results for first 6 images in the test set
y_test[:6]
```

Recurrent Neural Networks

Recurrent neural networks are used for sequential data analysis and prediction, especially in the finance, video analysis, and audio analysis domains. They can understand the context of the data and retain the information. Most traditional Machine Learning problems assume that the past values of the inputs are not related and are independent. But if you look at the aforementioned fields, you can see that the variables have relationships with their past values. The current stock price is related to the previous day's or month's stock price. The current word in a sentence depends on the word that came before.

This kind of data is called *time series data.* RNNs provide a way to effectively come up with computations that can predict the next sequence based on the sequence currently provided.

A simple RNN structure is provided in Figures 5-14 and 5-15.

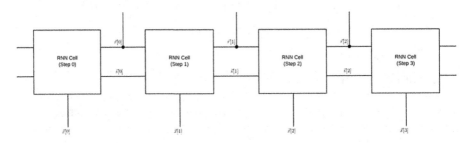

Figure 5-14. *Sequence of RNN cells (arXiv:1808.03314v4 [cs.LG] 4 Nov 2018)*

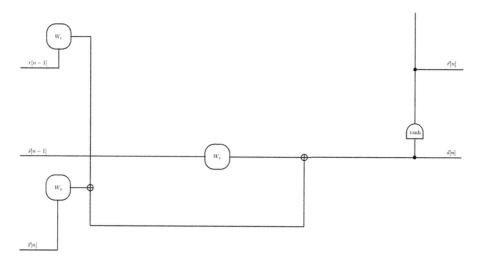

Figure 5-15. *Single RNN cell (arXiv:1808.03314v4 [cs.LG] 4 Nov 2018)*

Here is an explanation of the RNN notations used in the previous diagrams:

- S is the hidden state

- x is the input vector

- W is the weights

- r is the activated output

Let's now look at the entire process of an RNN cell. At timestep t, the RNN cell takes an input x. It also takes the value of the hidden state from the previous RNN cell. This helps RNN take into consideration the previous context and understand the new input. The new state (hidden) is calculated in this RNN by applying the Tanh activation function to the previous state and the input. In all the combined RNN cells, the weight matrix W is shared throughout the process.

```python
import pandas as pd
import numpy as np
import matplotlib.pyplot as plt
from keras.models import Sequential
from keras.layers import Dense, SimpleRNN

#Generating Random Data
t=np.arange(0,1000)
x=np.sin(0.02*t)+2*np.random.rand(1000)
df = pd.DataFrame(x)
df.head()

#Splitting into Train and Test set
values=df.values
train, test = values[0:800,:], values[800:1000,:]

# convert dataset into matrix
def convertToMatrix(data, step=4):
    X, Y =[], []
    for i in range(len(data)-step):
        d=i+step
        X.append(data[i:d,])
        Y.append(data[d,])
    return np.array(X), np.array(Y)

trainX,trainY =convertToMatrix(train,6)
testX,testY =convertToMatrix(test,6)
trainX = np.reshape(trainX, (trainX.shape[0], 1, trainX.shape[1]))
testX = np.reshape(testX, (testX.shape[0], 1, testX.shape[1]))

#Making the RNN Structure
model = Sequential()
model.add(SimpleRNN(units=32, input_shape=(1,6),
activation="relu"))
```

```
model.add(Dense(8, activation="relu"))
model.add(Dense(1))

#Compiling the Code
model.compile(loss='mean_squared_error', optimizer='rmsprop')
model.summary()

#Training the Model
model.fit(trainX,trainY, epochs=1, batch_size=500, verbose=2)

#Predicting with the Model
trainPredict = model.predict(trainX)
testPredict= model.predict(testX)
predicted=np.concatenate((trainPredict,testPredict),axis=0)
```

The problem with RNNs is that they suffer from the problems of vanishing and exploding gradients. You already know that RNNs are best suited for time series data. But imagine a body of text consisting of multiple paragraphs. In the first paragraph, the author tells the readers that she is talking about England. In all the subsequent paragraphs, she is talking about the same country, but doesn't reference the name of the country. As human readers, we understand that the country of interest is England, but for RNNs, this ambiguity may cause problems.

Neural networks learn from the concept of backpropagation. The process starts from the last layer of the neural network and can move up to the first layer. To move from one layer to another, backwards, you use the concept of matrix multiplication and linear algebra. This causes problems if the current value is too large or too small. If the values are <1, you keep on moving backward and the values keep shrinking until they vanish. This makes it impossible to learn from the data and the problem is called the *vanishing gradient problem*. Similarly, if the values are too large, they keep on getting larger and larger until they crash the model. This problem is called the *exploding gradient problem*.

To overcome these problems, you can use LSTM (long short-term memory) and GRUs (gated recurrent units). The following sections look at LSTM followed by GRUs.

Long Short-Term Memory

As mentioned, RNNs often fail to recall what was said long before. Consider this text:

> *"Since childhood, Shreya·was crazy about dance. She knows many different styles of dance. Mostly she does break dancing, but now she works in corporate. She works on Deep Learning."*

Shreya can dance which dance style?

This is where a recurrent neural network may not work! The reason behind this is the vanishing gradient problem. Once many words are fed in, this information gets lost somewhere. This problem can be solved by using a slightly modified version of RNN, which is known as LSTM (long short-term memory).

LSTM consists of the following components:

- Cell

- Cell state

- Hidden state

- Gates

A *cell* is a memory unit that stores the information. A cell also has the power to decide what to store and when to allow the reads. Hence, it gives LSTMs the power to selectively remember or forget things.

To make cells apply this decisive power, they are fed by two states: the cell state and the hidden state. The entire forgetting and remembering mechanism is done in LSTMs using something called *gates*. Gates are similar to the neural network nodes, wherein they either block the information or pass it. They do this by learning the weight and bias parameter from the information given as input. The weights are learned using the backpropagation approach. Figure 5-16 shows the architecture of LSTMs. Let's look at the components of LSTMs in a little more detail.

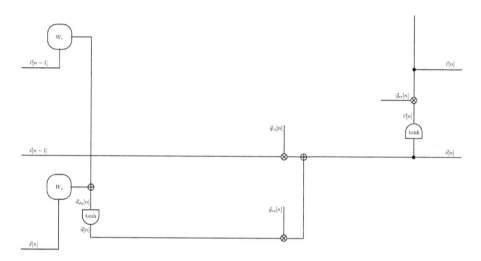

Figure 5-16. *Simple LSTM cell (arXiv:1808.03314v4 [cs.LG] 4 Nov 2018)*

The horizontal line running through the center of Figure 5-16, s, is considered the cell state. Values of the cell state can be changed using the following gates:

- Forget gate

- Input gate

- Output gate

Forget Gate

As the name suggests, if you want to remove some of the unnecessary information from a cell state, you use this gate. This decision is made by passing the past cell state and current input to a sigmoid function. The output is either a 0 or a 1. A value of 0 means forget the output and 1 means keep it. Hence, wherever the value is 0, that number is removed from the cell state matrix. Mathematical operations in this cell can be represented by:

$$f_t = \sigma\left(W_f.\left[h_{t-1}, x_t\right] + b_f\right)$$

Figure 5-17 shows these operations.

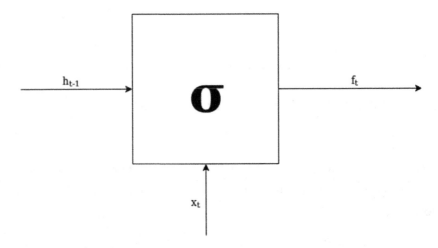

Figure 5-17. *Forget gate*

The next step is to decide what new information you're going to store in the cell state. This has two parts. First, a sigmoid layer called the input gate layer decides which values you'll update. Next, a Tanh layer creates a vector of new candidate values, Ct, that could be added to the state. In the next step, you combine these two to create an update to the state.

Input Gate

Once you have removed the trivial information, the next step adds the new information. First, a sigmoid function is used where you transfer the past cell state and the current input. This gives an output of 0 or 1. Wherever you get 1, that information is going to be passed to the new cell state. Next, you pass the same two inputs to a Tanh function. This helps you get all the possible information that can be added to a cell state. Finally, the Tanh and sigmoid outputs will be multiplied (using Hadamard multiplication) and the final output will be added to the cell state. This process is represented by following mathematical operations:

$$i_t = \sigma\left(W_i.\left[h_{t-1}, x_t\right] + b_i\right)$$

$$\tilde{C}_t = \tanh\left(W_c.\left[h_{t-1}, x_t\right] + b_c\right)$$

$$C_t = f_t * C_{t-1} + i_t \tilde{C}_t$$

Figure 5-18 shows all the operations.

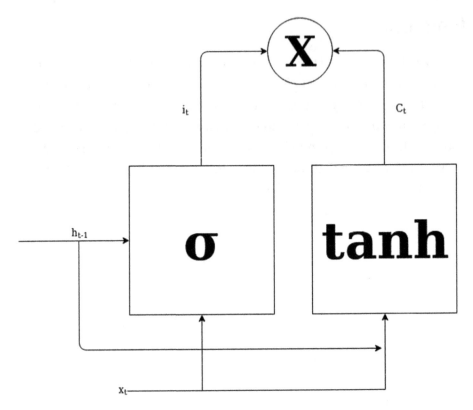

Figure 5-18. *Input gate*

Output Gate

In this gate, you first scale the values of the cell state to -1 and +1. This is done by passing the current state to a Tanh function. Next, you use the same sigmoid filter of the forget gate and apply it here. This helps to determine which values need to be outputted. A combination will give you the final output as well as the cell state input for the next LSTM cell. Mathematically, it's as follows:

$$o_t = \sigma\left(W_o.[h_{t-1}, x_t] + b_0\right)$$

$$h_t = o_t * tanh(C_t)$$

Figure 5-19 shows the operations of the output gate.

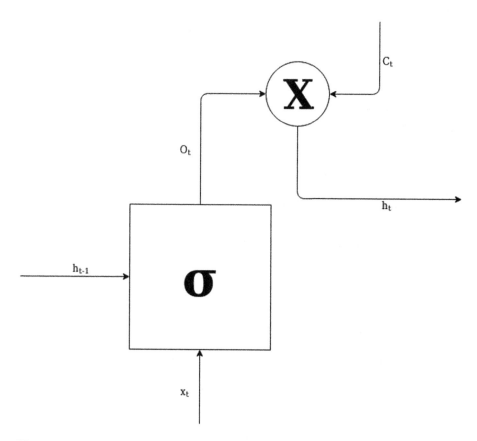

Figure 5-19. *Output gate*

The following is an example implementation of the same example used in RNN, but this time using LSTMs.

```
import pandas as pd
import numpy as np
import matplotlib.pyplot as plt
from keras.models import Sequential
from keras.layers import Dense, LSTM
```

```python
#Generating Random Data
t=np.arange(0,1000)
x=np.sin(0.02*t)+2*np.random.rand(1000)
df = pd.DataFrame(x)
df.head()

#Splitting into Train and Test set
values=df.values
train, test = values[0:800,:], values[800:1000,:]

# convert dataset into matrix
def convertToMatrix(data, step=4):
    X, Y =[], []
    for i in range(len(data)-step):
        d=i+step
        X.append(data[i:d,])
        Y.append(data[d,])
    return np.array(X), np.array(Y)

trainX,trainY =convertToMatrix(train,6)
testX,testY =convertToMatrix(test,6)
trainX = np.reshape(trainX, (trainX.shape[0], 1, trainX.
shape[1]))
testX = np.reshape(testX, (testX.shape[0], 1, testX.shape[1]))

#Making the LSTM Structure
model = Sequential()
model.add(LSTM(units=4, input_shape=(1,6), activation="relu"))
model.add(Dense(8, activation="relu"))
model.add(Dense(1))

#Compiling the Code
model.compile(loss='mean_squared_error', optimizer='rmsprop')
model.summary()
```

```
#Training the Model
model.fit(trainX,trainY, epochs=1, batch_size=500, verbose=2)

#Predicting with the Model
trainPredict = model.predict(trainX)
testPredict= model.predict(testX)
predicted=np.concatenate((trainPredict,testPredict),axis=0)
```

Another version of RNN that solves the vanishing and exploding gradient problem is called gated recurrent units (GRU). The next section discusses this architecture in detail.

Gated Recurrent Units

Similar to LSTMs, gated recurrent units also operate through gates, which help them overcome the problems that RNNs face. Figure 5-20 shows a simple structure of a GRU cell.

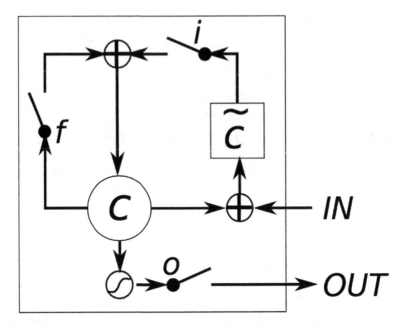

Figure 5-20. *Single GRU cell (LSTM Gating. Chung, Junyoung, et al. "Empirical evaluation of gated recurrent neural networks on sequence modeling." (2014))*

GRUs have only two gates as compared to LSTMs. These gates are:

- Reset gate

- Update gate

As with LSTMs, these gates also decide what information needs to be passed to the output. The next sections look at each gate's operation in a GRU cell.

Update Gate

This gate gives an output range of 0 to 1. This gate helps the model decide how much of the past information to pass to the future. If the model wants to, it can decide to copy all the information present in the previous time steps and hence eliminate the risk of a vanishing gradient descent. Here are the mathematical operations that are performed at this gate:

$$z_t = \sigma\left(W^{(z)}x_t + U^{(z)}h_{t-1}\right)$$

Figure 5-21 shows the operations of the update gate.

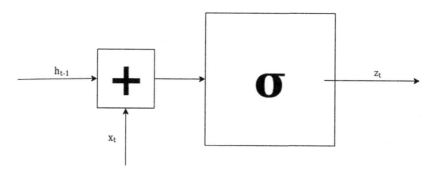

Figure 5-21. *Update gate*

Reset Gate

The reset gate has exactly the same structure as the update gate, which is shown in Figure 5-21. This gate tells the model about the information that needs to be forgotten from the past. This operation is performed by the following mathematical equation:

$$r_t = \sigma\left(W^{(r)}x_t + U^{(r)}h_{t-1}\right)$$

Figure 5-22 shows the operations of the reset gate.

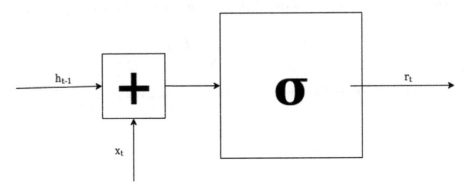

Figure 5-22. *Reset gate*

In a GRU cell, the reset gate is used to forget the past information. All the relevant information is stored in memory using the following equation (see Figure 5-23).

$$h'_t = tanh\left(Wx_t + r_t \odot Uh_{t-1}\right)$$

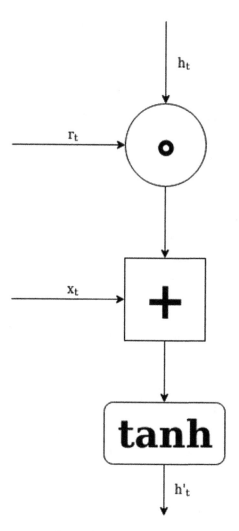

Figure 5-23. *Forgetting the information*

The update gate is applied to the output to determine the information that needs to be collected from the current memory. This can be achieved using the following mathematical equation:

$$h_t = z_t \odot h_{t-1} + \left(1 - z_t\right) \odot h_t'$$

This is the final output that is passed to the next GRU cell. Here's the application of GRU in Python.

```python
import pandas as pd
import numpy as np
import matplotlib.pyplot as plt
from keras.models import Sequential
from keras.layers import Dense, GRU

#Generating Random Data
t=np.arange(0,1000)
x=np.sin(0.02*t)+2*np.random.rand(1000)
df = pd.DataFrame(x)
df.head()

#Splitting into Train and Test set
values=df.values
train, test = values[0:800,:], values[800:1000,:]

# convert dataset into matrix
def convertToMatrix(data, step=4):
    X, Y =[], []
    for i in range(len(data)-step):
    d=i+step
    X.append(data[i:d,])
    Y.append(data[d,])
    return np.array(X), np.array(Y)

trainX,trainY =convertToMatrix(train,6)
testX,testY =convertToMatrix(test,6)
trainX = np.reshape(trainX, (trainX.shape[0], 1, trainX.shape[1]))
testX = np.reshape(testX, (testX.shape[0], 1, testX.shape[1]))

#Making the GRU Structure
model = Sequential()
```

```
model.add(GRU(units=4, input_shape=(1,6), activation="relu"))
model.add(Dense(8, activation="relu"))
model.add(Dense(1))

#Compiling the Code
model.compile(loss='mean_squared_error', optimizer='rmsprop')
model.summary()

#Training the Model
model.fit(trainX,trainY, epochs=10, batch_size=500, verbose=1)

#Predicting with the Model
trainPredict = model.predict(trainX)
testPredict= model.predict(testX)
predicted=np.concatenate((trainPredict,testPredict),axis=0)
```

This finishes the discussion of basic Deep Learning architectures. Before moving on to the next chapter, take a look at one live use case of LSTMs and GRUs. This example uses them to predict the closing price of a stock (Carriage Services Inc.). The code is applied to the Carriage Services Inc. Stock Price dataset, which you can download from the https://finance.yahoo.com/quote/CSV/history?p=CSV link.

```
import numpy
import pandas as pd
from keras.models import Sequential
from keras.layers import Dense, LSTM, GRU
from sklearn.preprocessing import StandardScaler
from sklearn.metrics import mean_squared_error
import math

# convert an array of values into a dataset matrix
def create_dataset(dataset, step=1):
    dataX, dataY = [], []
```

```
    for i in range(len(dataset)-step-1):
    a = dataset[i:(i+step), 0]
    dataX.append(a)
    dataY.append(dataset[i + step, 0])
    return numpy.array(dataX), numpy.array(dataY)

# load the dataset
dataframe = pd.read_csv('carriage.csv', usecols=[1])
dataset = dataframe.values
dataset = dataset.astype('float32')

# standardize the dataset
scaler = StandardScaler()
dataset = scaler.fit_transform(dataset)

# split into train and test sets
train_size = int(len(dataset) * 0.90)
test_size = len(dataset) - train_size
train, test = dataset[0:train_size,:], dataset[train_
size:len(dataset),:]

# Reshaping Data for the model
step = 1
train_X, train_Y = create_dataset(train, step)
test_X, test_Y = create_dataset(test, step)

train_X = numpy.reshape(train_X, (train_X.shape[0], 1, train_X.
shape[1]))
test_X = numpy.reshape(test_X, (test_X.shape[0], 1, test_X.
shape[1]))

# create and fit the LSTM network
model = Sequential()
model.add(LSTM(10, input_shape=(1, step)))
```

```
model.add(Dense(1))
model.compile(loss='mean_squared_error', optimizer='adam')
model.summary()
model.fit(train_X, train_Y, epochs=10, batch_size=50, verbose=1)

# create and fit the GRU network
model1 = Sequential()
model1.add(GRU(10, input_shape=(1, step)))
model1.add(Dense(1))
model1.compile(loss='mean_squared_error', optimizer='adam')
model1.summary()
model1.fit(train_X, train_Y, epochs=10, batch_size=50,
verbose=1)

# make predictions from LSTM
trainPredict = model.predict(train_X)
testPredict = model.predict(test_X)

# make predictions from GRU
trainPredict1 = model1.predict(train_X)
testPredict1 = model1.predict(test_X)

# invert predictions from LSTM
trainPredict = scaler.inverse_transform(trainPredict)
train_Y = scaler.inverse_transform([train_Y])
testPredict = scaler.inverse_transform(testPredict)
test_Y = scaler.inverse_transform([test_Y])

# invert predictions from GRU
trainPredict1 = scaler.inverse_transform(trainPredict1)
testPredict1 = scaler.inverse_transform(testPredict1)
```

```
# calculate root mean squared error for LSTM
print("*****Results for LSTMs*****")
trainScore = math.sqrt(mean_squared_error(train_Y[0],
trainPredict[:,0]))
print('Error in Training data is: %.2f RMSE' % (trainScore))
testScore = math.sqrt(mean_squared_error(test_Y[0],
testPredict[:,0]))
print('Error in Testing data is: %.2f RMSE' % (testScore))

# calculate root mean squared error for GRU
print("*****Results for GRUs*****")
trainScore1 = math.sqrt(mean_squared_error(train_Y[0],
trainPredict1[:,0]))
print('Error in Training data is: %.2f RMSE' % (trainScore1))
testScore1 = math.sqrt(mean_squared_error(test_Y[0],
testPredict1[:,0]))
print('Error in Testing data is: %.2f RMSE' % (testScore1))
```

Summary

This chapter discussed artificial neural networks. To understand the concepts of Fuzzy Neural Networks, a foundation of neural networks is necessary. This chapter set that foundation. You learned about how a typical ANN operates and the role of backpropagation and forward propagation for learning the patterns. Then you looked at the specific applications of neural networks in computer vision, through convolutional neural networks, and natural language processing, through recurrent neural networks. Finally, you looked at some of the disadvantages met by RNNs and how LSTMs and GRUs try to address these issues. You looked at the practical aspects of all these architectures using Python.

The next chapter covers some of these Fuzzy Neural Networks and related algorithms in detail.

CHAPTER 6

Fuzzy Neural Networks

In the previous chapters, you saw neural networks based on crisp inputs, weights, parameters, etc. But in real-life applications, it's not necessary that you always get the same kind of inputs. *Fuzziness* in neural networks results in networks having Fuzzy Signals, Fuzzy Weights, etc., in which case you are dealing with *Fuzzy Neural Networks.* This chapter looks at the different architectures of Fuzzy Neural Networks and the components that define them. You will later learn about the Adaptive Neuro Fuzzy Architecture and its different versions.

Fuzzy Neural Networks are used to find the parameters related to a Fuzzy System by learning them through the given data, with the help of neural networks. These parameters can be Fuzzy Sets, Fuzzy Rules, Fuzzy Membership Functions, etc. Simple Fuzzy Neural Networks have the following properties:

- A Fuzzy Neural Network is based on a data-driven approach using the methodology of neural networks.

- Fuzzy Neural Networks can be made with or without the prior knowledge of the Fuzzy Rules, as they can be learned from the data parallel using neural networks.

© Himanshu Singh, Yunis Ahmad Lone 2020
H. Singh and Y. A. Lone, *Deep Neuro-Fuzzy Systems with Python*,
https://doi.org/10.1007/978-1-4842-5361-8_6

- The properties of the underlying Fuzzy System are maintained throughout, even though the parameters are learned along the way.

- A Fuzzy System can be represented as having multiple nodes, as shown in Figure 6-1.

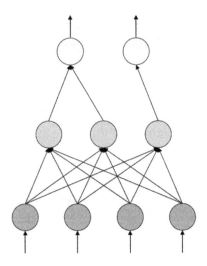

Figure 6-1. *Fuzzy Neural System*

a. The first layer is the input layer

b. The second layer represents the Fuzzy Rules

c. The third layer contains the output nodes

If you have normal Neural Networks and apply some Fuzzy Set Operators like Max and Min (T-Norm and S-Norm) to them, they are an extension and are called *Hybrid Neural Networks.* You will learn about the Hybrid Neural Networks in the next section.

Why would you use use Fuzzy Neural Networks when Fuzzy Systems are capable of doing the task? Fuzzy Systems are used to find the relationship between the input and output domain. This is defined by a set of rules (Fuzzy Rules). But what if you cannot capture all the rules that may be present in the system? To solve this issue, you can have a neural network-based system where you learn different rules based on the membership functions and then make the entire architecture.

In a nutshell, you can say that if you have data, you can find Neuro Fuzzy Systems out of it using Fuzzy Neural Networks. Also, if you already have a Fuzzy System, you can enhance and optimize it using the same approach. Let's start the chapter by first covering Fuzzy Neurons and their architecture.

Fuzzy Neurons

The previous chapter talked about normal neural networks. Neurons are the core component of artificial neural networks and they are used to compute some operations. They take some values as inputs and then perform some kind of operations over them to give a processed output.

Figure 6-2 represents one of the simple neurons showing a basic operation. In the diagram, you can see that there are two inputs and based on that, we are defining an output, called *y*. *w1* and *w2* are the weights that we learn and, based on that, we take a weighted sum as an output.

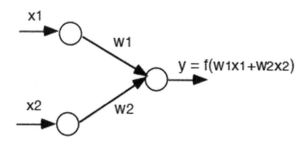

Figure 6-2. *Fuzzy Neuron*

This diagram doesn't have any of the core components of a neural network architecture, like hidden layers or activation functions, but it can still be considered a simple neural network. Therefore, the output can be expressed as follows:

$$y = f(w1\, x1 + w2x2)$$

The function f can be of any type. It can be nothing, or you can add an activation function like Sigmoid or Relu. Note that we are using a normal mathematical operation like addition. If you use operators like addition, subtraction, or activation functions like Sigmoid or Relu, this neural network is called a *regular neural net*. But instead, if you apply Fuzzy Operators like T-Norm or S-Norm, it is called a *hybrid neural net*. It is a Fuzzy Architecture and has different signals, weights, and functions in a classical set format. You can apply different operations of T-Norm and T-Co-Norm to the inputs and weights later. One processing unit of a Hybrid Neural Net is called a *Fuzzy Neuron*.

Let's look at the different types of Fuzzy Neurons in a Hybrid Neural Net architecture. Figures 6-3 and 6-4 show these neurons specific to T-Norm and T-Co-Norm operations.

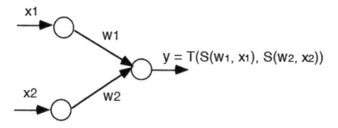

Figure 6-3. *T-Norm operation*

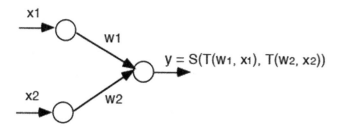

Figure 6-4. *T-Co-Norm operation*

In Figure 6-3, you can see that it's doing a T-Co-Norm operation followed by T-Norm. Figure 6-4 shows the exact opposite. This specific operation of applying one continuous function to the output of another continuous function comes under the domain of a *Fuzzy Neuron*. So the first diagram (Figure 6-3) represents **an** *AND-Fuzzy Neuron* and the second one (Figure 6-4) is an *OR-Fuzzy Neuron,* where:

$$Y_{AND} = T\left(S\left(w_1,x_1\right),S\left(w_2,x_2\right),\ldots,S\left(w_n,x_n\right)\right)$$

$$Y_{OR} = S\left(T\left(w_1,x_1\right),T\left(w_2,x_2\right),\ldots,T\left(w_n,x_n\right)\right)$$

You have already seen in previous chapters that the Fuzzy Systems consist of membership functions. The AND or OR Fuzzy Neuron basically operates on the membership values obtained from the MFs. Since you have to learn the values of w1 and w2 in the diagram, they will directly relate to the output of the system. This means that if the weights are very high, then in the case of OR neurons, the input will strongly affect the output. In the case of AND neurons, the input will weakly affect the output. Here are some other neurons used in Fuzzy Neural Networks:

- Implication-OR Neuron

- Kwan and Cai's Neuron

  - K&C's Max Neuron

  - K&C's Min Neuron

Let's review how these neurons operate. Figure 6-5 shows the Implication-OR Neuron. This neuron has an implication operator applied between the input x and the weight w. After that, it applies the Triangular Co-norm operator on the output.

In the neuron shown in Figure 6-5, you have an implication.

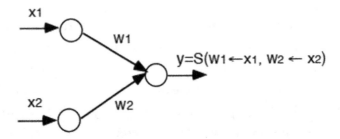

Figure 6-5. Implication-OR neuron

Next is a series of K&C neurons (see Figure 6-6).

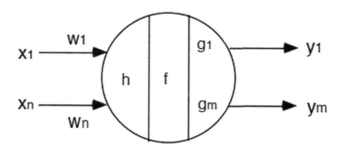

Figure 6-6. *K&C neuron*

Kwan and Cai's Fuzzy Neurons have a somewhat complex structure. First, for each input x, we multiply it by its learned weight, w. Once you do this for all the input nodes, you aggregate them and convert them into one single input. Next, you find the state of this input, which can be represented by:

$$s = f(z - \theta)$$

In this equation, you use *f* as the selected activation function, while θ represents the activation threshold. Finally, you get the output by applying a function to the state. Let's apply the concept to two types of K&C Fuzzy Neurons: K&C Max neurons (see Figure 6-7) and Min neurons (see Figure 6-8).

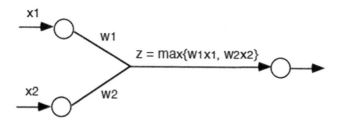

Figure 6-7. *K&C Max neuron*

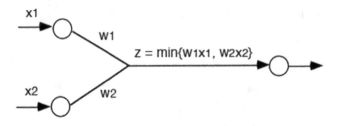

Figure 6-8. K&C min neuron

The K&C Max neuron uses the T-Co-Norm operation, while the K&C Min neuron uses the T-Norm operation.

You'll keep on learning about Fuzzy Neurons throughout the chapter.

Fuzzy Inference Neural Networks

Just by the name, you can say that if you combine the concept of Fuzzy Inference Systems and Neural Networks, FINN (Fuzzy Inference Neural Networks) is born. Before going through a detailed analysis of FINNs, you need to first understand their types. Basically, FINNs can be placed into the following categories:

- Cooperative FINNs

- Concurrent FINNs

- Integrated/Fused FINNs

When you have training data and use the neural networks to find the membership functions and Fuzzy Rules, this comes under the domain of Cooperative FINNs (see Figure 6-9).

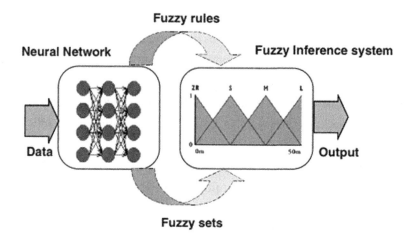

Figure 6-9. *Cooperative FINNs*

When you are not able to measure the input variables directly, then instead of using Cooperative FINNs, you use Concurrent FINNs. In this process, neural networks continuously help the FIS so that the final system is always the best. Figure 6-10 shows a concurrent FINN where the input data is fed to a neural network, which helps determine the best membership functions to be processed by the Fuzzy Systems later. Combining neural networks with Fuzzy does not optimize the Fuzzy Systems, but improves the overall performance of the system.

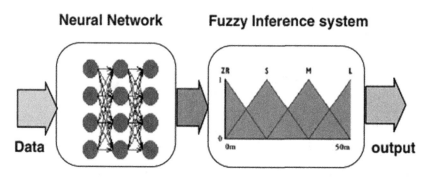

Figure 6-10. *Concurrent FINNs*

207

Integrated FINNs are used to find the parameters of FIS. Say you have a common shared database that stores knowledge representations and data structures. This database is shared between the neural network and the Fuzzy Inference System. Neural networks and Fuzzy Inference Systems have some disadvantages of their own. But when you combine both concepts, you get integrated FINNs, which result in much more efficient architectures.

Now that you know the categories of Fuzzy Inference Neural Networks, it's time to look at some of the most popular FINNs used in the domain. We'll discuss the following architectures:

- Fuzzy Associative Memories

- Mamdani Integrated FINNs

- Takagi-Sugeno Integrated FINNs

Fuzzy Associative Memories

Before learning about Fuzzy Associative Memories, you must first know what the name *associative memory* means. Any associative memory has a primary task of storing the input and output patterns and also the relationship and mapping between them. The major task is to find an output pattern when an incomplete or noisy input pattern is provided.

An associative memory can be represented by the following equations:

$$a = \{(x_i, y_i)\mid i = 1,2,3\ldots n\}$$

$$G(x_i) = y_i$$

In the previous equations, a represents the finite set of associations where x is the input pattern and y is the output pattern. G(x) is a function that defines the mapping between x and y. Some of the terminology related to associative memories is as follows

- Fundamental memory set

- Fundamental memory

- Auto-associative memory

- Hetero-associative memory

- Recording phase

- Associative mapping

- Neural associative memory

- Fuzzy associative memory

All the associations present, which is $a = \{(x_i, y_i) \mid i = 1,2,3...n\}$, are called the *fundamental memory set,* while each association, $(x_i \text{ and } y_i)$, is called a *fundamental memory.* When the association is related to itself, it is called *auto-associative memory,* but if it is different, then it's called *hetero-associative memory.* Therefore, $a = \{(x_i, x_i) \mid i = 1,2,3...n\}$ is an auto-associative memory, but $a = \{(x_i, y_i) \mid i = 1,2,3...n\}$ is a hetero-associative memory.

The process of finding the function G(x) is called the *recording phase,* whereas G is called *associative mapping.* When the associative mapping is a neural network, it is called **neural associative memory** and when it is a Fuzzy Neural Network, it's called *Fuzzy Associative Memory.* In a Fuzzy Associative Memory, the input and output patterns are Fuzzy Sets.

Generally, a Fuzzy Associative Memory (FAM) is a Fuzzy Inference Neural Network that stores a rule in the system. This rule is a Fuzzy Rule with the following format:

"If x is x_k then y is y_k"

Fuzzy Associative Memories can be of two types:

- Max-Min Fuzzy Associative Memory

- Max-Product Fuzzy Associative Memory

Since a Fuzzy Associative Memory is a Fuzzy Neural Network, their main component is Fuzzy Neurons. The two FAMs differ in terms of the types of neurons. If a FAM contains a Max-C_M neuron, then it is called a Max-Min FAM, but if it contains a Max-C_P neuron, it's called a Max-Product FAM. A Max-C Fuzzy Neuron can be represented by the following equation:

$$y = \left[\vee_{j=1}^{n} C\left(w_j, x_j\right) \right] \vee \theta$$

In the previous equation, C represents the Fuzzy Conjunction Operation, while θ denotes the bias. If this neuron has the maximum operation applied, it is called a Max-C_M neuron, whereas if a product operation is applied, it's called a Max-C_P neuron.

Mamdani Integrated Finns

Mamdani Integrated FINNs (also known as Mamdani Integrated Neuro Fuzzy Systems) use the method of backpropagation to learn the parameters of a membership function. In this method, you try to find the best values of a parameter by minimizing a cost function. Recall that Chapter 5 discussed the backpropagation method. Because this method utilizes the concept of backpropagation, it comes under the domain of supervised learning methods.

Figure 6-11 shows how a Mamdani Integrated FINN looks.

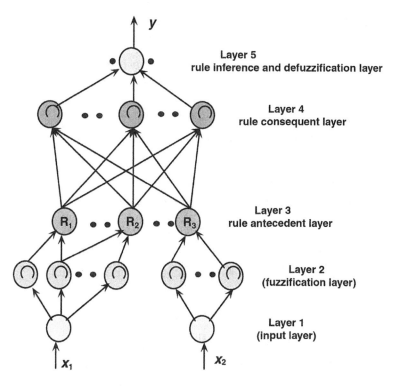

Figure 6-11. *Mamdani Integrated FINNs*

The architecture of Mamdani Integrated FINNs consists of five layers:

- *Layer 1:* This layer consists of the direct inputs, hence it's called the *input layer*. Each node in this layer consists of individual inputs that are passed directly to the next layer's nodes.

- *Layer 2:* This is also called the *fuzzification layer*. Here you convert the crisp inputs passed from the input layer into Fuzzy Sets. It tries to find the degree of membership of each individual input value in the

211

Fuzzy Set. Fuzzy Clustering approaches are used to define the number and type of membership functions for each input variable. Throughout the process of backpropagation, the membership function's numbers and types will keep on changing to fine-tune the entire system.

- *Layer 3:* This layer is used to define the antecedents of the rule base. Therefore, this layer is called the *rule antecedent layer.* Each node in this layer uses the T-Norm operation. The output of this layer is the firing strength of the corresponding Fuzzy Rule.

- *Layer 4:* This layer is called the *rule consequent layer.* As the name suggests, it is used to determine the consequents for each rule antecedent. It helps to define the membership of each antecedent to the output value. The number of nodes in this layer are equal to the number of rules in the previous layer.

- *Layer 5:* This is the final *defuzzification layer.* In this layer, all the rule consequents are combined using the T-Co-Norm operation and then they are converted into crisp outputs using the defuzzification approaches.

Takagi Sugeno Integrated FINNs

In this method, the propagation happens in two steps. These two steps require a combination of backpropagation and mean least squares estimation. The first method is used to fine-tune the membership functions, whereas the second method is used to find the parameters. Figure 6-12 shows the diagram that represents a Takagi Sugeno FINN.

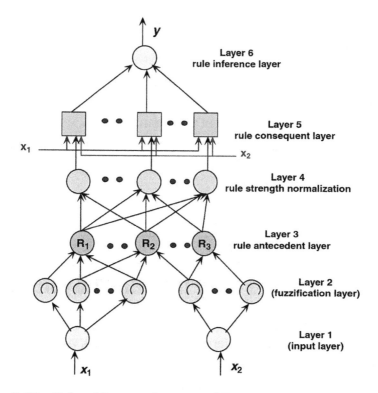

Figure 6-12. *Takagi Sugeno integrated FINNs*

Layer 1 is the input layer. It passes the crisp inputs directly to the second layer. Layer 2 converts the crisp inputs received into Fuzzy Sets. Layer 3 finds the antecedents of the Fuzzy Rules. These three layers work exactly similar to the Mamdani FINNs.

Layer 4 is used to determine each rule's firing strength and then normalize it. This is done by finding each rule's firing strength and then dividing it by the sum of all the rules' firing strengths. This can be represented by this formula:

$$\underline{w_i} = \frac{w_i}{\sum_{i=1}^{n} w_i}$$

213

Layer 5 is used to determine the consequents of the rule using the least squares method. This is done using this formula:

$$\underline{w}_i f_i = \underline{w}_i \left(p_i x_1 + q_i x_2 + r_i \right)$$

In this equation, p, q, i represent the parameter sets.

Layer 6 is used to aggregate all the outputs coming from the previous layer. This can be represented by:

$$Output = \frac{\sum_{i=1}^{n} w_i f_i}{\sum_{i}^{n} w_i}$$

Adaptive Neuro Fuzzy Inference Systems

Chapter 4 discussed Sugeno and Tsukamoto Fuzzy Inference Systems. Using Adaptive Neuro-Fuzzy Inference System (ANFIS), you can represent both the Sugeno and Tsukamoto systems. That's why it is named an *adaptive network,* as with one network, you can represent multiple networks with minor changes.

You can also represent Mamdani FIS using ANFIS, but that requires a complex mathematical approach and is out of the scope of this book. This chapter discusses the Sugeno and Tsukamoto approaches using ANFIS. The example will use a system with two inputs and one output, for the sake of the understanding.

ANFIS Representing Sugeno FIS

The Sugeno Fuzzy Inference System (FIS) rules take the following format, as discussed in previous chapters:

If x is A1 and y is B1 then f1 = p1x+q1y+r1

If x is A2 and y is B2 then f2 = p2x+q2y+r2

Figure 6-13 is the result of representing these two rules graphically using the Sugeno approach. Chapter 3 discussed this concept in detail.

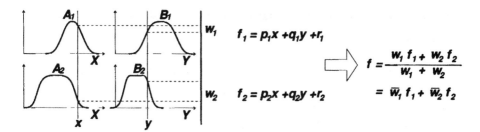

Figure 6-13. *Sugeno defuzzification*

Figure 6-14 shows the structure of ANFIS representing the same architecture of Sugeno.

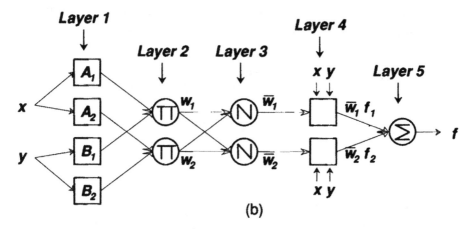

Figure 6-14. *ANFIS based on Sugeno*

We cover this architecture layer-wise in the following sections.

Layer 1: Membership Function Layer

This layer is a combination of membership functions for each input. If you look at the rules, you know that the inputs x and y are defined by the membership functions A1, A2, B1, and B2. These functions can be represented by:

$$A1 = \mu_{A1}(x)$$
$$A2 = \mu_{A2}(x)$$
$$B1 = \mu_{B1}(y)$$
$$B2 = \mu_{B2}(y)$$

Layer 2: Antecedent Layer

In this layer, you define the antecedent for the rules. All the signals that are coming to this layer generate the output for them by finding the product of them. This can be represented by:

$$w_1 = \mu_{A1}(x) . \mu_{B1}(y)$$
$$w_2 = \mu_{A2}(x) . \mu_{B2}(y)$$

In this layer, you use the T-Norm operator.

Layer 3: Normalization Layer

Here you normalize the antecedent layer output, which can also be referred to as *Normalized Firing Strength*. To normalize the past layer output, you divide it by the overall firing strength. This can be represented as follows:

$$\underline{w}_1 = w_1 / (w_1 + w_2)$$

$$\underline{w}_2 = w_2 / (w_1 + w_2)$$

Layer 4: Consequent Layer

In this layer, you deal with the consequent of the rule. In Sugeno, you saw the consequent of the rules. In this layer, you must generate similar output.

$$\underline{w}_1 f_1 = \underline{w}_1 \left(p_1 x + q_1 x + r_1 \right)$$

$$\underline{w}_2 f_2 = \underline{w}_2 \left(p_2 x + q_2 x + r_2 \right)$$

In the previous equations, p, q, r represent the parameter set.

Layer 5: Aggregation Layer

Once you get the consequent layer outputs where you included different parameter sets, in this layer you find the aggregate of all the outputs of the previous layer. This operation can be represented by this equation:

$$\sum_i^n \underline{w}_i f_i = \frac{\sum_i^n \underline{w}_i f_i}{\sum_i^n \underline{w}_i}$$

ANFIS Representing Tsukamoto FIS

In the Tsukamoto FIS, you get the consequent as follows:

$$f = \frac{w_1 f_1 + w_2 f_2}{w_1 + w_2}$$

Figures 6-15 and 6-16 show diagrams representing the defuzzification process for the Tsukamoto FIS and its ANFIS counterpart.

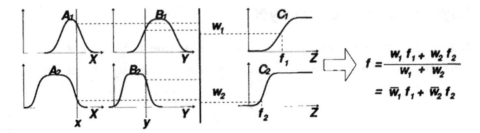

Figure 6-15. *Tsukamoto defuzzification*

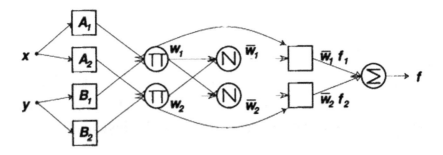

Figure 6-16. *ANFIS based on Tsukamoto*

As you can see in Figure 6-16, the system is similar to that of a Sugeno-based ANFIS, only instead of using a linear membership function, a weighted membership function is used. Therefore, all the layers remain exactly the same as with the Sugeno-based example, but in the last layer the defuzzification equation changes.

Let's look at the application of ANFIS using Python. In Python, there is a package named anfis that you can use to apply the concept of ANFIS. The dataset contains three columns. The first two columns define the crisp inputs, while the last column defines their fuzzified values. This example uses the ANFIS to predict these fuzzified values and checks the error of the model. You can install the anfis package by writing the following command:

```
pip install anfis
```

Here is the code applied to a dummy dataset:

```python
# Importing necessary libraries
import anfis
from anfis.membership import membershipfunction, mfDerivs
import numpy
training_data = numpy.loadtxt("training.txt", usecols=[1,2,3])
X = training_data [:,0:2]
Y = training_data [:,2]
# Defining the Membership Functions
mf = [[['gaussmf',{'mean':0.,'sigma':1.}],['gauss
mf',{'mean':-1.,'sigma':2.}],['gaussmf',{'mean':-
4.,'sigma':10.}],['gaussmf',{'mean':-7.,'sigma':7.}]], [['gau
ssmf',{'mean':1.,'sigma':2.}],['gaussmf',{'mean':2.,'sigma':3
.}],['gaussmf',{'mean':-2.,'sigma':10.}],['gaussmf',{'mean':-
10.5,'sigma':5.}]]]
# Updating the model with Membership Functions
mfc = membershipfunction.MemFuncs(mf)
# Creating the ANFIS Model Object
anf = anfis.ANFIS(X, Y, mfc)
# Fitting the ANFIS Model
anf.trainHybridJangOffLine(epochs=20)
# Printing Output
print(round(anf.consequents[-1][0],6))
print(round(anf.consequents[-2][0],6))
print(round(anf.fittedValues[9][0],6))
# Plotting Model Performance
anf.plotErrors()
anf.plotResults()
```

Figure 6-17 shows how, in each iteration, better membership functions are defined, which means that the error is reduced at each iteration. Figure 6-18 shows how the predictions fall in comparison to the actual data.

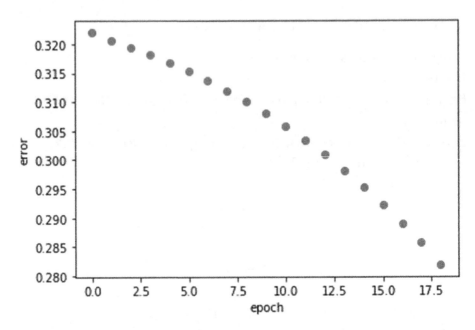

Figure 6-17. *Reduction of error in each epoch*

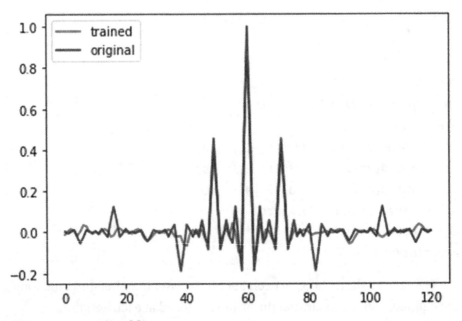

Figure 6-18. *Fitted line*

Summary

This chapter looked at some of the architectures of Fuzzy Neural Networks. You saw how a simple FINN is composed of a Fuzzy Neuron and then explored various kinds of neurons. Then you explored various FINN architectures, starting with Fuzzy Associative Memories to the Sugeno Integrated FINN. Finally, you saw how an Adaptive Neuro Fuzzy Inference System (ANFIS) works and looked at its application using Python.

The next chapter looks at some of the advanced concepts related to Fuzzy Neural Networks.

CHAPTER 7

Advanced Fuzzy Networks

This chapter looks at some of the advanced Fuzzy Networks.
Figure 7-1 shows a classic Neuro Fuzzy System. But before you get too
far, it's important to know some of the core components that are used
in building these systems. This chapter starts by discussing the Fuzzy
Clustering method. Then it moves on to genetic algorithms and wraps
up by reviewing the most commonly used architectures belonging to the
domain of advanced Fuzzy Networks.

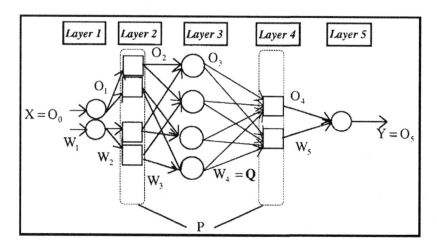

Figure 7-1. *Neuro-Fuzzy Inference System*

© Himanshu Singh, Yunis Ahmad Lone 2020
H. Singh and Y. A. Lone, *Deep Neuro-Fuzzy Systems with Python*,
https://doi.org/10.1007/978-1-4842-5361-8_7

This chapter begins by discussing Fuzzy Clustering—their requirements and their applications.

Fuzzy Clustering

Clustering is a method you use to group data into a few categories, based on the similarities present. These categories are termed *clusters* (see Figure 7-2).

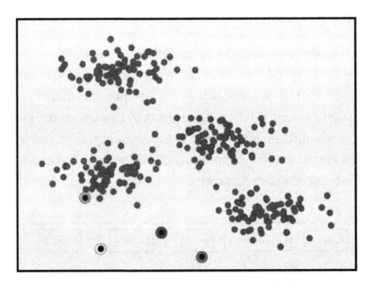

Figure 7-2. *Clustering*

Machine Learning uses different methods for clustering, such as K-Means Clustering, Hierarchical Clustering, DBScan, and so on. Similarly, when we talk about Fuzzy Networks, there are methods like Fuzzy C-Means Clustering, Gaussian Application to find clusters, and so on. This chapter discusses Fuzzy C-Means Clustering in detail.

Fuzzy C-Means Clustering

Suppose I have a set of data points, X, which I want to put into a k number of clusters based on some similarity metrics. In the form of a set, suppose the data looks like the following:

$$X = \{x_1, x_2, x_3, \ldots x_m\}$$

To divide them into k number of clusters using the C-Means Clustering approach, the first thing that you do is randomly take k number of points from the data. Assume that these k points are the centroids (see Figure 7-3).

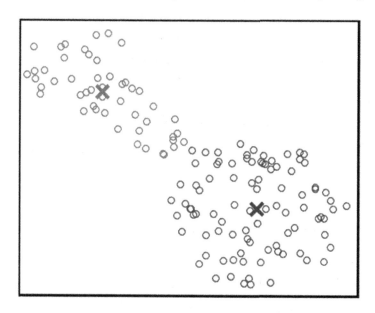

Figure 7-3. *C-Means Clustering*

Using the Manhattan or Euclidean distance, you then find out that all the remaining points are closer to the cluster centroid point. This is how you get the first set of data assigned to k number of clusters. But you started by randomly selecting k points and calling them *centroids*. In reality, they are not. Therefore, you need to continue the process to rectify this assumption.

Euclidean Distance

A normal straight-line distance between any two points is called a *Euclidean Distance*. To get this distance, you use the following formula:

$$d = \sqrt{\left(q_1 - p_1\right)^2 + \left(q_2 - p_2\right)^2}$$

In the next step, you find the actual centroids of the clusters that you defined. Once you find that, some of the points may lose the original membership of that cluster. They may now be much closer to another cluster, as compared to the cluster that they were originally part of. Hence, you start reassigning these points based on the new centroids. This will help you get a revised k number of clusters with new member points. Again, you find the new centroid and repeat the process. You keep on repeating the process until the new clusters don't make the points move from one cluster to another.

Let's look at the entire algorithm mathematically:

1. Define N data points that need to be clustered:

    $$x_i, where\ i = 1,2,3...N$$

2. Assume the number of cluster to be made is represented by C, where $2 \leq C \leq N$

3. Define the cluster fuzziness represented by f, where $f > 1$

4. Define a membership matrix U having dimension of $N \times C \times M$. This matrix should be defined randomly following these conditions:

    a. $U_{ijm} \in [0,1]$, and

    b. $\sum_{i=1}^{n} U_{ijm} = 0$ for each i and fixed value of m.

5. Determine the cluster centers. This can be done by using the following equation:

$$CC_{jm} = \frac{\sum_{i=1}^{N} U^{f}_{ijm} x_{im}}{\sum_{i=1}^{N} U^{f}_{ijm}}$$

where j represents the cluster and m represents the dimension.

6. Calculate the Euclidean Distance. You can find this equation by using the following equation:

$$D_{ijm} = \left\| \left(x_{im} - C_{jm} \right) \right\|$$

where i represents data point, j represents cluster, and m represents dimension

7. After finding the Euclidean Distance, you have to update the membership matrix defined in Step 4 with the new value. This can be done by using the following equation:

$$U_{ijm} = \frac{1}{\sum_{c=1}^{D} \left(\frac{D_{ijm}}{D_{icm}} \right)^{\frac{2}{f-1}}}$$

We apply the above equation only for the data points where $D_{ijm} > 0$. If $D_{ijm} = 0$ then we have full membership and the value initialized is 1.0

8. Repeat the Steps 1 to 5 until the value of $U < \in$, where $\in$ is the termination criteria.

Applications of Fuzzy C-Means Clustering

You can use Fuzzy C-Means Clustering for the following use cases and domains:

- When image processing, especially when clustering objects present inside the image. Used with image-based segmentation as well.

- Used with swarm intelligence.

- Used with remote sensing.

Python Implementation of Fuzzy C-Means

The following code contains two sets of data—train and test data. With the help of train data, you can find the final centroid of the clusters, while after that you should use the test data to check in which cluster the new data points are allocated. This example uses the Python Package called fuzzycmeans. You can install it using this command:

```
pip install fuzzycmeans
```

If the package shows a problem in execution, you can clone the GitHub repository, then copy the two Python files—fuzzy_clustering. py and visualization.py—to your home directory and then run the code. Make sure to install the bokeh package before running the code, as it is a dependency for this Fuzzy C-Means package. You can install it by writing the following:

```
pip install bokeh
```

This package is an implementation of the paper "FCM: The Fuzzy C-Means Clustering Algorithm" by James C. Bezdek, Robert Ehrlich, and William Full. You can view and clone the source code as well, by going to the GitHub repository at https://github.com/oeg-upm/fuzzy-c-means.git.

This example uses the AirlinesCluster dataset. You can find this dataset in the GitHub repository of this book. Alternatively, you can download it from the Kaggle website. The example uses only two columns—Balance and BonusMiles—to start clustering. You can use all the columns and visualize the output if you want.

```
import pandas as pd
import numpy as np
import numpy as np
import logging
from fuzzy_clustering import FCM
from visualization import draw_model_2d
from sklearn import preprocessing

dataset = pd.read_csv("AirlinesCluster.csv") #Importing the
airlines data

dataset1 = dataset.copy() #Making a copy so that original data
remains unaffected

dataset1 = dataset1[["Balance", "BonusMiles"]][:500] #Selecting
only first 500 rows for faster computation

dataset1_standardized = preprocessing.scale(dataset1)
#Standardizing the data to scale it between the upper and lower
limit of 1 and 0

dataset1_standardized = pd.DataFrame(dataset1_standardized)

fcm.set_logger(tostdout=False) #Telling the package class to
stop the unnecessary output

fcm = FCM(n_clusters=5) #Defining k=5

fcm.fit(dataset1_standardized) #Training on data
```

```
predicted_membership = fcm.predict(np.array(dataset1_
standardized)) #Testing on same data

draw_model_2d(fcm, data=np.array(dataset1_standardized),
membership=predicted_membership) #Visualizing the data
```

Fuzzy Adaptive Resonance Theory

In Fuzzy C-Means Clustering, you saw that based on the distance between the points, you can group them into clusters. But what if you can control this similarity between the points in one cluster? Fuzzy Adaptive Resonance Theory (Fuzzy ART) provides the power to control the similarity between the data points inside a cluster. Therefore, Fuzzy ART is another approach to find the best clusters by controlling the similarity between them.

A lot of data is given to a Fuzzy ART model. This data contains a lot of patterns from which Fuzzy ART tries to extract the similarities. It finds the best adaptive clusters from the new data, based on the data that trained the model. One thing to notice in this model is that even though you train it on the input data, it doesn't contain any hidden layers like other Fuzzy Architectures.

A Fuzzy ART Architecture mainly contains two components:

- Attention

- Orientation

Attention helps Fuzzy ART define the clusters or categories that it finds are the best, based on the data. *Orientation* helps it determine whether all the clusters that are found are valid. This means it helps Fuzzy ART accept or reject a category defined by attention. That's why this is called an *adaptive architecture.* One more reason for the name adaptive is its ability to adapt to new data. Whatever patterns are learned from the training data, new data can be allocated to any one of the clusters. But if the new data does not resemble any existing clusters, Fuzzy ART has the power to create a new cluster that's totally different from an existing cluster.

Fuzzy ART is used for clustering and classification problems, and the input data that it takes can be discrete or continuous. Some of the features related to the Fuzzy ART Architecture are:

- The entire architecture has only one weight. Hence, it is easier to manage and update.

- It can process both binary and non-binary data.

- It contains the following important hyperparameters:

  - *Vigilance threshold*:

    This threshold generally decides the memory of a Fuzzy ART. It helps determine the final number of clusters. It is used to perform the attention operation.

  - *Choice parameter*:

    This is used to determine which cluster to keep and which should not be validated. If the threshold is surpassed, the cluster is selected; otherwise, it's rejected. It's used to perform the orientation operation.

  - *Learning rate*:

    Used to determine patterns in the input data.

Figure 7-4 shows the basic Fuzzy ART Architecture.

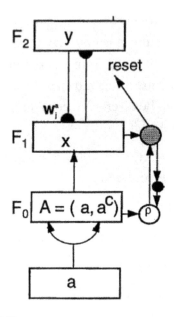

Figure 7-4. *Fuzzy ART*

As you can see, there are three layers in Fuzzy ART. The last layer is called the *output layer* and it is fully connected to the second layer. As you may recall from an earlier chapter on neural networks, a fully connected layer is a layer where each node is connected to all the nodes present in the previous or next layer. Therefore, in Fuzzy ART, the F2 and F1 layers are fully connected. In the first layer, you take m-dimensional input and, before passing it to the next layer, you multiply it by its complement. This makes the number of nodes present in the F1 layer 2m-dimensional. Finally, the output layer talks to the second layer continuously to decide whether the cluster formed is valid. If it's valid, the outcome is 1; otherwise, it's 0.

$$y_j = \begin{cases} 1, & \text{When node is active in Output layer} \\ 0, & \text{Otherwise} \end{cases}$$

The next sections look at the operations of each layer in a little detail.

Layer 1: F_0 (Orienting Layer)

This layer takes the input fuzzy pattern, finds the complement of it, and then passes both the original and complemented input to the next layer. This operation can be summarized by this equation:

$$I = (a, a_c) = (a_1, a_2, ..., a_n, 1 - a_1, 1 - a_2, ..., 1 - a_n)$$

There is a Reset node that's also present in this layer and it takes input from all the layers and helps transform the input patterns received.

Layer 2: F_1 and F_2 (Attentional Layer)

Since the complemented input is also passed to the F_1 layer, the number of nodes present is the double of the input layer, represented by $2n$ nodes. The F_2 layer contains m nodes. Both layers are connected by connection weights, represented by W_i and w_j. W_i represents the connection from F_1 to F_2, while w_j represents the connection from F_2 to F_1. These weights can be represented by the following mathematical equations:

$$W_i = W_1, W_2, ..., W_{2n}$$
$$w_j = w_1, w_2, ..., w_{2n}$$

In the F_2 layer there are two kinds of nodes: committed and uncommitted. A *committed node* is a node where the value of the weight matrix should be 1; otherwise, it is called an uncommitted node. This can be represented by the following equation:

$$node = \begin{cases} committed, & if\ w_j = w_j(0) = (1,1,...,1) \\ uncommitted, & otherwise \end{cases}$$

Input of F_2 layer can be defined as,

$$t(i)=\begin{cases} \dfrac{|I|}{a_x+M_x}, & \text{for an uncommted node} \\ \dfrac{|I \wedge w_j|}{a_x+|w_j|}, & \text{for a committed node} \end{cases}$$

Fuzzy ARTMAP (see Figure 7-5) is an advanced application of Fuzzy ARTs. It is a supervised learning approach that can be used in different applications. It contains two Fuzzy ART components, called Fuzzy ART_x and Fuzzy ART_y, whereas the third component contains the inter-ART relationship. Covering Fuzzy ARTMAPs is outside the scope of this book, Figure 7-5 shows the architecture of a Fuzzy ARTMAP for your reference.

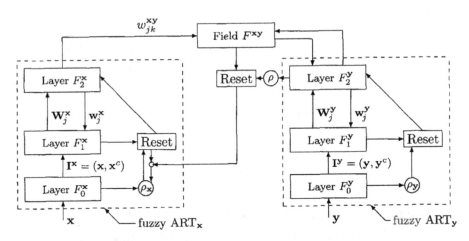

Figure 7-5. *Fuzzy ARTMAP*

Applications of Fuzzy ART

- Used in finding pattern recognition

- Used to handle time series data

- Used to monitor the quality of products

Python Implementation of Fuzzy ART

IRIS is a dataset collected by Edgar Anderson. It quantifies the morphological variations in Iris flowers. Based on their variations, the flowers are divided into three categories. This example uses Fuzzy ART to look at the morphological data and cluster the Irises based on their similarity.

The algorithm is quite complex, so in the code repository, you can find FuzzyART.py file. Just upload it in your home folder and run the following code.

```python
from functools import partial
import numpy as np
import FuzzyART as f
import sklearn.datasets as ds

l1_norm = partial(np.linalg.norm, ord=1, axis=-1)#Used for
regularization so that we can penalize the parameters that are
not important

if __name__ == '__main__':

    iris = ds.load_iris()#load the dataset in the python
    environment

    data = iris['data'] / np.max(iris['data'],
    axis=0)#standardize the dataset

    net = f.FuzzyART(alpha=0.5, rho=0.5) #Initialize the
    FuzzyART Hyperparameters

    net.train(data, epochs=100) #Train on the data

    print(net.test(data).astype(int)) #Print the Cluster Results

    print(iris['target']) #Match the cluster results
```

Genetic Algorithms

Genetic algorithms are groups of search algorithms that follow the biological process of natural selection and its genetics. The general principle of natural selection says that the fittest individuals are selected (by surviving) to produce the offspring of the next generation.

When you define a search problem, you first determine a few variables to use to make search decisions. These variables are called *decision variables*. The first step involves finding these variables and then encoding them to finite-length strings of alphabets.

Once you represent these variables in an encoded strings format, they are called *chromosomes*. Individual alphabets inside the string are called *genes,* while the value that they are storing is called an *allele*. For example, suppose a person wants to go from one place to another. The different routes that he can take are the decision variables. He can encode them using strings and then these routes may be called *chromosomes*. The individual cities along the route may be called *genes*.

Once you have to find out different types of solutions, you can represent them as a set. This set is called a *candidate solution* set. It is a collection of different chromosomes. Once you have all these solutions, the next step is to decide which ones are the best and which ones to avoid. Genetic algorithms use different mathematical models and computer simulations to differentiate between the good and bad chromosomes.

There is an ideal number of chromosomes present inside a candidate solution. If you have too few, you'll get a substandard solution. But if you have too many, it may lead to unnecessary computations. Figure 7-6 shows the flowchart representing the process of genetic algorithm-based searching.

Figure 7-6. *Genetic algorithm steps*

The *Initialization* step involves a random generation of a candidate solutions set. In the second step, *Evaluation*, you try to find a fitness value for each chromosome and then assign it to the determined value. The next four steps are used to generate more chromosomes in the candidate solution set using different methods. When you select the chromosomes with high fitness values and make copies of them, that is the *Selection* step. When you combine multiple chromosomes to get a better chromosome, this step is called *recombination*. When you try to modify the current candidate solution's property, it's called *mutation*. Lastly, when the new solutions replace the older ones, it is called *replacement*. You will repeat this process until a specific threshold is reached.

Selection

One of the most famous methods in selection is *tournament method.* Once you have a candidate solution set, you select k members from it and run a tournament among them. The fittest member after the tournament is considered to be selected. This process continues several times to get the best members. An individual's chance to participate in a tournament is called *selection pressure.* An entire algorithm of the tournament method is illustrated in Figure 7-7 and can be summed up by these points:

1. Select k individuals from the population and perform a tournament amongst them.

2. Select the best individual from the k individuals.

3. Repeat Steps 1 and 2 until you have a desired population size.

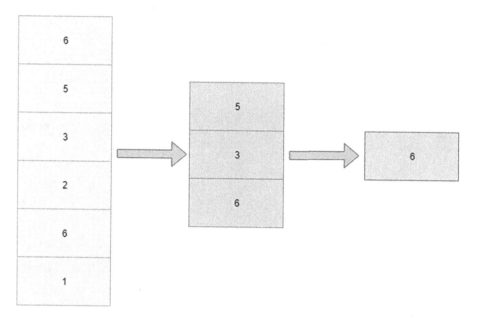

Figure 7-7. *Tournament selection*

Recombination

In recombination, you use *crossover methods* to find the fittest members. Using the *one-point crossover* method (see Figure 7-8), you first select two chromosomes. You randomly select any one point in the two chromosomes and then exchange the genes present after that point. *Two-point crossover* (see Figure 7-9) involves randomly selecting two points in the two chromosomes. The section between the two points is later exchanged.

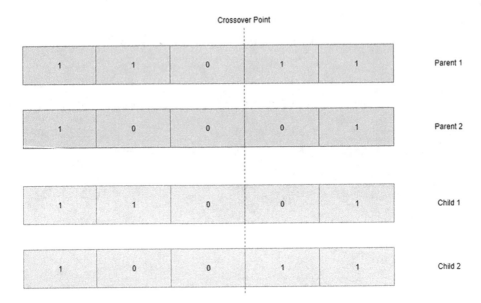

Figure 7-8. *One-point crossover*

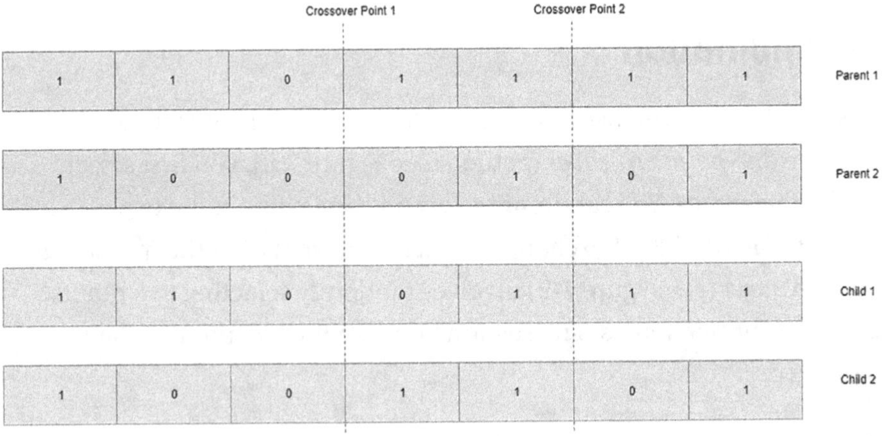

Figure 7-9. *Two-point crossover*

Apart from these two methods, you also have uniform crossovers and arithmetic crossover. In uniform crossover, the combination is random between the two parents. This means any feature can randomly be selected from either parent. In arithmetic crossover, any mathematical operation can be applied to the two parents to give you the resulting offspring. Figures 7-10 and 7-11 show uniform crossover and arithmetic crossover having binary operations.

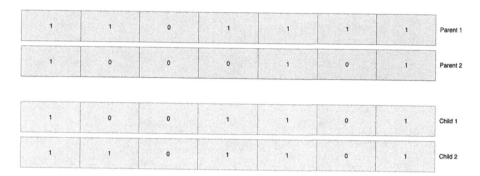

Figure 7-10. *Uniform crossover*

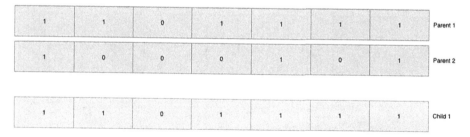

Figure 7-11. *Arithmetic crossover*

Mutation

As discussed, in mutation you try to change the property of chromosomes to check whether they become fit. In the *Flipping* (*Bit Flip Mutation*) method, genes are changed to their opposites. If a chromosome contains 0 and 1, then the 0s are flipped to 1 and vice versa. The second method is *Interchanging* (*Swap Mutation*), where you select any two points in a chromosome and then the genes at those positions are interchanged. In *Reversing* (*Inversion Mutation*), you select a random point and the genes after that point are reversed, just like the flipping method. If, from the entire chromosome, a subset of genes is selected and then shuffled randomly, this is called a *scramble mutation*. Figures 7-12 through 7-15 illustrate these concepts of mutation.

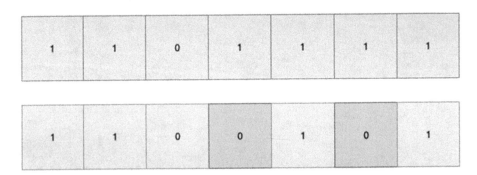

Figure 7-12. *Bit flip mutation*

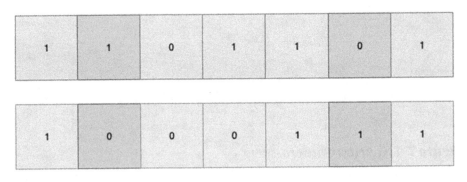

Figure 7-13. *Swap mutation*

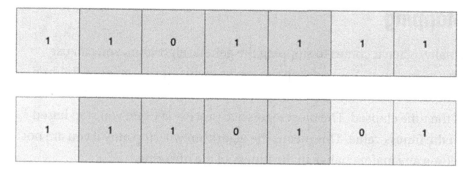

Figure 7-14. *Inversion mutation*

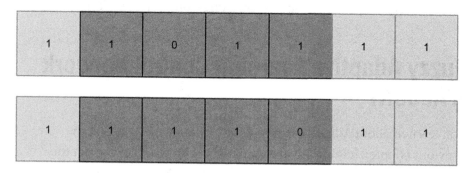

Figure 7-15. *Scramble mutation*

Replacement

If a child is fitter, you randomly select two less fit parents in the population and replace them with the children. This is called *random replacement*. This can be subdivided into *weak parent replacement* and *both parents replacement*. In weak parent replacement, only the weaker parent is replaced, while in the latter method, both parents are replaced.

Stopping

Finally, when it comes to stopping the genetic algorithm, you can use several methods. You can stop the process when the number of children generated crosses a threshold. You can also stop based on the threshold of the time elapsed. The most regressive process is when you stop based on the fitness value. This means the algorithm will stop only if you are not getting any major change in the fitness of the offspring.

Now that you have learned about the basics required for discussing the advanced Fuzzy Architecture, let's continue this chapter by discussing the first architecture—Fuzzy Adaptive Learning Control Network (FALCON).

Fuzzy Adaptive Learning Control Network (FALCON)

You learned about Adaptive Neuro-Fuzzy Inference Systems in the previous chapter. It takes advantage of neural networks to predict the Fuzzy Output based on the Fuzzy Inputs. FALCON uses the power of genetic algorithms and Fuzzy Clustering to learn the patterns from the input and then predict the output.

To construct a FALCON network automatically, you use a hybrid algorithm, and it's called *FALCON-GA* (FALCON Genetic Algorithm). To construct the network, FALCON-GA requires the following steps:

- Fuzzy Clustering

- Genetic algorithm

- Backpropagation

This section uses the Fuzzy Clustering approach to find the clusters in the input and output spaces using the training data. Then it uses genetic algorithms to find the Fuzzy Rules by looking at the association between the input and the output clusters found in the first step. Finally, the backpropagation method will fine-tune the membership functions of the input and output variables. Figure 7-16 shows a FALCON network generated using FALCON-GA.

Figure 7-16 shows a proposed FALCON in the paper by Cheng-Jian Lin and Chin-Teng Lin (1997). This architecture consists of five layers. Layer 1 is the input layer. Layer 2 defines the membership functions of the input nodes from the previous layer. Layer 3 consists of a Fuzzy Rulebase derived from the first two layers. Layer 4 helps in deriving the consequents of the Fuzzy Rules.

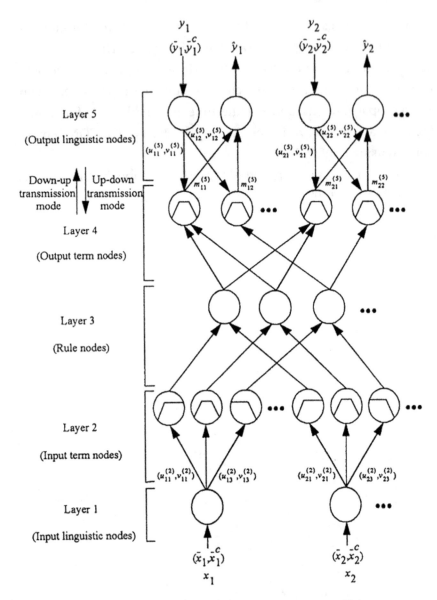

Figure 7-16. *Proposed FALCON (Cheng-Jian Lin, & Chin-Teng Lin. (1997), an ART-based fuzzy adaptive learning control network. IEEE Transactions on Fuzzy Systems, 5(4), 477–496. doi:10.1109/91.649900)*

Finally, in Layer 5, you get the output, which is then compared to the desired output, and fed back in.

Neuro-Fuzzy Systems for Classification of Data (NEFCLASS)

NEFCLASS is a special class of Fuzzy Perceptron. It has a total of three layers. In between each layer is where weight transfer happens. These weights are Fuzzy Sets, while in the hidden layers, each node represents a Fuzzy Rule. The output layer explains the patterns of classes.

The model is trained on the input data to find a rule that segregates similar patterns into several classes. Hence, NEFCLASS is a supervised learning approach, where the error is minimized using backpropagation.

The NEFCLASS rulebase follows this structure:

$$If\ x_1\ is\ \mu_1\ and\ x_2\ is\ \mu_2...and\ x_n\ is\ \mu_n$$

$$then\ (x_1, x_2,...x_n)\ belongs\ to\ Class\ i$$

NEFCLASS can be used to learn the structure of these rules from the training data and then learn the shape of their membership functions. For each input x_i, there can be q_i Fuzzy Sets and k rules. The output of the NEFCLASS can be represented by:

$$\varphi(x) = \{c_1, c_2, ..., c_n\}$$

Figure 7-17 provides an example NEFCLASS structure. It divides two inputs into two output classes with the help of five Fuzzy Rules.

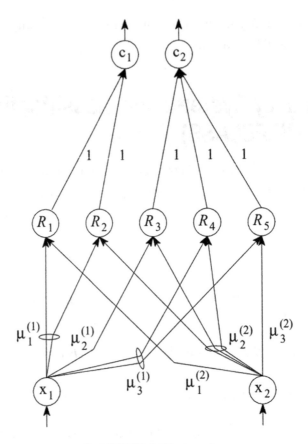

Figure 7-17. *An example NEFCLASS structure*

Fuzzy Inference Software (FINEST)

The FINEST tool is used to build a Fuzzy Knowledge-based system, developed by the Laboratory of International Fuzzy Engineering (LIFE). FINEST consists of a small processing component called a *unit* (see Figure 7-18). Units are used to represent knowledge. Their main task is to take the input, process it in a specific way, and produce some output. The following is a list of units in FINEST, based on usage:

- Rule units

- Function units

- External units

- Memory units

- Composite units

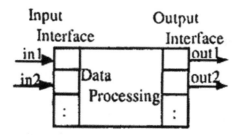

Figure 7-18. *View of a unit*

Rule Unit

Rule units contain one or more Fuzzy Rules. They are used for the inference of the input data. The result is output through the rule unit's output inference.

Function Unit

This unit uses LISP for processing. It takes input data, evaluates it, and then outputs the evaluated value. It has some configurable parameters for the task of fine-tuning. The major use of a functional unit is for the defuzzification process.

External Unit

This unit is an executable UNIX file. It is an inconfigurable component. The computations that are done are in the form of a UNIX process.

Memory Unit

This unit is used to store the status of a system. It is used to store the intermediate results as well. Different units talk with this unit and extract the values.

Composite Unit

When multiple units are combined, they are called a *composite unit* (see Figure 7-19). They are used to build a complete hierarchical system.

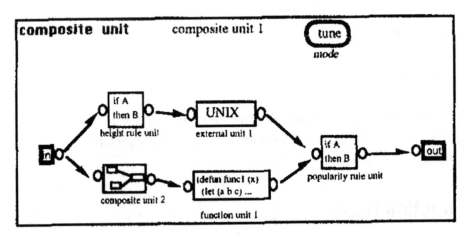

Figure 7-19. *Structure of a composite unit (Tano, S., Miyoshi, T., Kato, Y., Oyama, T., Arnould, T., Bastian, A., & Umano, M. (n.d.). Fuzzy inference software-FINEST: overview and application examples, doi:10.1109/fuzzy.1995.409810)*

Some of the problems that FINEST can solve are these:

- Sometimes rules may represent vague meanings.

- Finding the best and suitable implication operator is difficult.

- It is difficult to combine the inference results of different processes.

- It's difficult to do tuning automatically.

FINEST can be used to develop Fuzzy Systems or it can be used to quantify the fuzzy meaning of sentences.

Summary

This chapter looked at some of the advanced applications of Fuzzy Neural Networks. It discussed some of the current work happening in the research domain. It also looked at genetic algorithms, which are combined with Fuzzy Neural Networks to make some very good models. The chapter also looked at some of the applications of the algorithms in Python.

Index

A

© Himanshu Singh, Yunis Ahmad Lone 2020
H. Singh and Y. A. Lone, *Deep Neuro-Fuzzy Systems with Python*,
https://doi.org/10.1007/978-1-4842-5361-8

Printed in the United States
By Bookmasters